Portuguese-Americans
and Contemporary Civic Culture
in Massachusetts

Portuguese-Americans
and Contemporary Civic Culture
in Massachusetts

Clyde W. Barrow, Editor

University of
Massachusetts
Dartmouth

FUNDAÇÃO
LUSO-AMERICANA

Copy Donated by
Center for Portuguese Studies and Culture
and the Center for Policy Analysis
University of Massachusetts Dartmouth
North Dartmouth, Massachusetts
2002

PORTUGUESE IN THE AMERICAS SERIES

General Editor: Frank Sousa
Editorial Manager: Gina Reis
Copyeditor: Richard Larschan and Gina Reis
Graphic Designer: Spencer Ladd

Sponsored by the Center for Portuguese Studies and Culture with
generous financial assistance from the Luso-American Foundation.

Portuguese-Americans and Contemporary Civic Culture in Massachusetts/edited
by Clyde W. Barrow

Printed in the United States of America

Library of Congress Cataloging-in-Publication Data

Portuguese-Americans and contemporary civic culture in Massachusetts / Clyde
W. Barrow, editor.

p. cm.—(Portuguese in the Americas series)
Includes bibliographical references (p.)
ISBN 0-9722561-0-5
1. Portuguese Americans—Massachusetts—Politics and government.
2. Portuguese Americans—Massachusetts—Social conditions. 3. Portuguese
Americans—Massachusetts—Economic conditions. 4. Political culture—
Massachusetts. 5. Massachusetts—Politics and government—1951-
6. Massachusetts—Social conditions. 7. Masssachusetts—Ethnic relations. I.
Barrow, Clyde W. II. University of Massachusetts Dartmouth. Center for
Portuguese Studies and Culture. III. University of Massachusetts Dartmouth.
Center for Policy Analysis. IV. Series.

F75.P8 P67 2002

Contents

Acknowledgements

Acknowledgements

The chapters that comprise this book were the collective effort of many people, including individuals whose names do not appear as authors. The project was conceived by Dr. Frank Sousa, Director of the Center for Portuguese Studies and Culture (CPSC) at the University of Massachusetts Dartmouth. The generous financial support of the CPSC, as well as Dr. Sousa's enthusiastic moral support, insured that this project was launched, executed, and completed in late 1999 and early 2000. The book was co-sponsored by the Luso-American Foundation and benefited from the support of Representative Robert Correia and the entire Portuguese-American delegation to the Massachusetts State Legislature.

The study of Portuguese-Americans in Taunton, Massachusetts (Chapter 2) was initiated by Massachusetts State Senator Marc Pacheco, who is also a recipient of Portugal's Prince Henry the Navigator Award. Senator Pacheco's leadership in the Luso-American Citizenship Project of Taunton helped facilitate the project and insure its successful completion. The research presented in Chapter 2 was also supported by a small grant from the Luso-American Citizenship Project of Taunton.

Luis Dias, a former research assistant at the University of Massachusetts Dartmouth Center for Policy Analysis, was diligent and professional in conducting the interviews that constitute such an important part of our study of the Portuguese in Taunton. Diane Pimentel conducted the research on Portuguese language instruction at colleges and universities in Massachusetts included in Chapter 6. Dr. Rita Marinho, Dean of Arts and Sciences at Millersville University, and Pedro Bicudo read drafts of the manuscript and their suggestions have greatly improved the final document.

CHAPTER I

WHO ARE THE PORTUGUESE?:
THE POLITICAL CULTURE OF PORTUGUESE-AMERICANS
IN SOUTHEASTERN MASSACHUSETTS

CLYDE W. BARROW

The Portuguese in Southeastern Massachusetts

There are large concentrations of Portuguese-Americans in the towns and cities of Southeastern Massachusetts. Yet there has been little scholarly effort to study the political and civic behavior of Portuguese-Americans in a region where their political and cultural influence is potentially significant (see Figure 1). Southeastern Massachusetts consists of 48 cities and towns in Bristol, Plymouth, and Norfolk Counties. The region is 1,224 square miles in area and has a population of 949,520 (U.S. Census 1990). The major cities in the region, which account for about 39 percent of the region's population, are Attleboro, Brockton, Fall River, New Bedford, and Taunton. The so-called "Portuguese Archipelago" of Southeastern Massachusetts, covering an area of 511 square miles, includes eighteen cities and towns in Bristol and Plymouth Counties, with Fall River, New Bedford, and Taunton comprising more than half (58.3%) of the area's 415,896 population.

More than one-third (35.7%) of the residents in this ethnic archipelago are primarily of Portuguese heritage. Approximately 48.5 percent of Fall River's residents, 43.1 percent of New Bedford's residents, and 39.8 percent of Dartmouth's residents claim Portuguese as their primary ancestry.[1] When secondary ancestry is taken into account, this percentage rises to 52.9 percent for Fall River (4.3 percent secondary), 47.8 percent for New Bedford (4.7 percent secondary), and 44.9 percent for Dartmouth (5.1 percent secondary).[2] Other Southeastern Massachusetts communities, including Fairhaven, Taunton, Somerset, Berkley, Dighton, Westport, Freetown, and Acushnet also report significant numbers of residents who are of single Portuguese ancestry. Several towns on Cape Cod and Martha's Vineyard likewise have significant concentrations of Portuguese-Americans, including Provincetown, Truro, Tisbury, and Oak Bluffs.[3]

Portugal historically has one of the highest emigration rates in Europe. Portuguese immigrants from the Azores, Madeira, and the Cape Verde islands have arrived in the United States since the early 1800's when they began boarding American whaling vessels, which they used as stepping stones to the United States. U.S. immigration figures do not distinguish among the various origins of Portuguese immigrants, but it is estimated that 80 percent of Portuguese immigrants in the United States are Azoreans.[4] Portuguese immigration to the United States occurred in three major waves (1850-1870, 1890-1910, 1950-1980) related to economic factors in Portugal. Cultural factors including the attraction of the "American Dream" and Portuguese rituals of family reunification also drew significant numbers of Portuguese to the United States (see Figure 2).[5]

The first recorded group of Portuguese immigrants arrived in the United States in 1820. The majority of these immigrants were Azorean men who worked on American whaling vessels. An expanding whaling industry and poor living conditions in the Azores increased the level of Portuguese immigration during the 1860's and 1870's, which was the heyday of the u.s. whaling trade.[6] Azorean migration to the United States accelerated in the early 1900's as social networks developed between native Azoreans and friends and family members who resided in America.[7] These social networks played a major role in determining where Portuguese immigrants settled in the United States. Much of the first wave of Portuguese immigration was concentrated in a number of Southeastern Massachusetts communities, where immigrants soon found employment in the region's booming textile, apparel, and fishing industries.[8] By 1900, Massachusetts temporarily surpassed California in having the largest Portuguese population in the country.

Portuguese immigration began to slow in the 1920's partly due to new u.s. immigration policies, which purposely restricted immigration from southern Europe by establishing literacy requirements and a quota system. The Portuguese government also imposed restricitons on emigration beginning in World War I to keep young men in the country for military service. Substantial Portuguese immigration would not occur

FIGURE 1

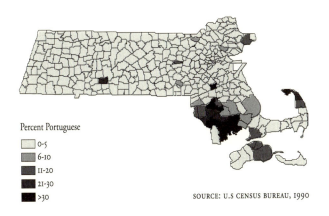

Percent Portuguese

0-5
6-10
11-20
21-30
>30

SOURCE: U.S CENSUS BUREAU, 1990

FIGURE 2

PORTUGUESE IMMIGRATION BY COUNTRY OF LAST RESIDENCE

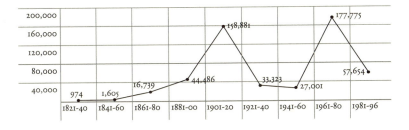

TABLE 1

THE PORTUGUESE OF THE UNITED STATES, 1990

Primary Ancestry Portuguese

State	Number	Percent of State Total
California	275,492	1.0%
Connecticut	35,523	1.2%
Massachusetts	241,173	4.3%
New Jersey	56,928	0.8%
New York	34,455	0.2%
Rhode Island	76,773	8.2%
All Other States	179,716	0.1%
Total:	900,060	15.8%

SOURCE: U.S. CENSUS BUREAU, 1990

again until the 1960's when the U.S. Immigration and Nationality Act of 1965 eliminated the quota system and replaced it with a system of preferential categories. The Act gave immigration preference to the spouses, siblings, siblings' spouses, and siblings' children of u.s. residents who applied to enter the United States. These preferences were used heavily by Portuguese immigrants for the purpose of family reunification.[9] Following this change in u.s. immigration policy, at least 177,775 Portuguese immigrants arrived in the United States and, by 1975, the number of immigrants arriving from Portugal exceeded that of every other country in Europe.[10] Portuguese immigration to the United States slowed considerably after the Revolution of the Carnations in 1974, although the United States is still one of the world's largest hosts to Portuguese immigrants. The u.s. Census estimates that there were 900,060 persons of Portuguese ancestry in the United States in 1990. The majority of Portuguese are concentrated in only six states (see Table 1).

While there are major bodies of scholarly work in political science, sociology, and ethnic studies that analyze the political behavior and attitudes of African-Americans, Latinos, Asian-Americans, and many other racial and ethnic groups,[11] the potentially significant political and civic role of Portuguese-Americans in selected areas of the country has received very little attention from scholars in these fields.[12] Despite the relative dearth of empirical information on Portuguese-Americans' political and civic participation, there are many commonly held assumptions about this group, which may or may not be true. For instance, it is often asserted that:

(1) Portuguese-Americans are less politically active than other ethnic groups.
(2) Portuguese-Americans have low levels of political knowledge and a high level of distrust in government.
(3) Portuguese-Americans do not have a distinctive political identity comparable to that of many other ethnic and racial groups.

Furthermore, local journalists, public officials, educators, and others offer several reasons to support the most commonly held assumptions about Portuguese-Americans. For example, it is commonly asserted that because Portugal was governed by an authoritarian dictatorship from 1926 to 1974, Portuguese immigrants do not have a history of political participation and therefore have failed to develop a democratic civic culture. Life under an authoritarian dictatorship is said to have fostered high levels of distrust in government, and this aversion to "politics" leads to low levels of political knowledge and creates a cultural disincentive to become citizens of the United States. It is assumed that many Portuguese immigrants intend to return to their home country and thus they do not place any importance on becoming citizens or on participating in the American political process. For the same reasons, however, it is often argued that Portuguese-Americans are more involved in "non-political" civic associations such as churches, nationality groups, fraternal organizations, and athletic clubs.

Moreover, there is an unusually high percentage of first-generation Portuguese-Americans in Southeastern Massachusetts with low levels of formal educational attainment. Consequently, a significant number of Portuguese-Americans, like the members of many other immigrant groups, have been employed in low-skill and low-paying jobs.[13] In general, it is well-established in the academic literature on political behavior and political sociology that low levels of political participation are strongly correlated with low educational attainment and low incomes.[14] Thus, in contrast to explanations that invoke a sort of historical or cultural determinism to explain Portuguese-American political behavior, other explanations invoke well-established sociological explanations based on their current socio-economic status.

Another factor that may encourage non-participation in the u.s. political process is the existence of vibrant ethnic enclaves among Portuguese-Americans. Many Portuguese, especially in Southeastern Massachusetts' urban areas, reside in ethnic neighborhoods where Portuguese is commonly spoken, where they have access to Portuguese language television, radio, and newspapers, and where they can find employment with little interaction outside their established ethnic boundaries. Since the existence of these enclaves does not encourage Portuguese-Americans to become fluent in English, they remain isolated from the u.s. political process, which is conducted mainly in English.

While such views often pass as conventional wisdom, in many respects they are merely ethnic legends derived from anecdotes, specula-

13

tion, and cultural stereotypes. This collection of essays treats such claims as hypotheses rather than facts. The major purpose of the studies that form the bulk of this collection of essays is to determine the actual levels of political and civic participation among Portuguese-Americans,[15] as well as their sense of political efficacy, their rates of satisfaction with their position in the local economy, and their attitudes on major cultural and social issues in the United States.[16] A final survey measures Portuguese language instruction in the public schools, colleges, and universities of Massachusetts.

Political and Civic Participation

Political participation is defined as any activity by private citizens that is more or less directly aimed at influencing the selection of government officials, the decisions they make, or the actions they take on public policy issues.[17] Political participation includes activities such as voting, lobbying, contributing to campaigns, writing or calling a public official, writing letters to the newspaper, calling talk radio shows, persuading friends to vote for a particular candidate, and being active in private organizations for political purposes. *Civic participation* is defined as any activity by private citizens that brings them into contact with other citizens for the purpose of pursuing common ends. Civic participation includes political activity, but it also includes participation in other private organizations that establish and transmit community, civic, or cultural values, including churches, business organizations, labor unions, athletic clubs, and fraternal organizations, among others.

The study of political and civic participation is important to understanding American politics and civic culture for several reasons.[18] First, political and civic participation by citizens are the essence or *sine qua non* of a vibrant democracy. Second, political and civic participation are important aspects of building a healthy local, regional, and national civil society—now often called social capital—through organizations that include political parties, labor unions, parent-teacher organizations, sports clubs, fraternal organizations, political action committees, churches, and many other institutions that bring citizens into contact with one another.[19] By participating in this diverse array of civic institutions, people influence the goals, values, and resource allocations of the

entire community—whether local, regional, or national. Finally, participation is not only important because it communicates citizens' preferences to government officials, but because it generates other psychic
benefits that reinforce democratic institutions. Participation provides a
sense of membership in the democratic community, a sense of satisfaction or mutual trust, and a sense of efficacy when civic action is successful. Participation is also an educational mechanism that teaches the civic
virtues of a democratic society (e.g., freedom of press, speech, lawful
assembly, rule by law, rotation in office, etc.). Thus, political and civic
participation is both a means to an end (representation) and an end-in-
itself (democracy).

For these reasons, there is considerable debate among scholars,
journalists, and public officials about the quality of American democracy, which numerous studies have documented is plagued by declining levels of political and civic participation. Concerned individuals
routinely lament "the decline of American civic culture" or "the collapse of American community," particularly in a country that lauds
itself as a model of democratic government. However, a wide array of
statistics and surveys demonstrates that Americans are disaffected with
politics and government. They are also less and less likely to participate
in the private institutions of civil society, which provide the foundation
for community interaction and political participation. For example,
the United States has the lowest voter turnout among the 22 established democracies.[20] The percentage of voting-age Americans voting in
Presidential elections has fallen from 61.9 percent in 1964 to 49.0 percent in 1996, while voter turnout in off-year U.S. Congressional elections has fallen from 58.5 percent in 1960 to 32.9 percent in 1998.[21]
More people did not vote in the 2000 Presidential election than voted
for either of the two major candidates. The decline in civic and political participation by Americans is accompanied, not surprisingly, by
declines in the sense of political efficacy.

Political Efficacy

Political efficacy is the degree to which individuals believe they can influence the political process, including decision-making by government
officials. Levels of political efficacy are highest when citizens feel that

15

they have an impact on political outcomes and when they believe the political system is responsive to their concerns. Many studies have also found an important link between levels of political efficacy, trust in government, and political knowledge.[22]

National public opinion surveys in the United States reveal declining levels of confidence in virtually all major institutions, including government at all levels, corporations and labor unions, and even organized religion. For example, fewer than a third of Americans say that they "trust the government in Washington to do what is right" most of the time, as compared to the 1960s, when three-quarters of Americans expressed trust in the federal government.[23] Only miniscule numbers of Americans now indicate that they have a "great deal of confidence" in the u.s. Congress (3.4%), the federal government (5.2%), state government (4.1%), local government (5.4%), and political organizations and parties (3.8%). At the same time, the percentage of Americans who agree with the statement that "public officials don't care what people think" has increased from 35 percent in 1958 to 62 percent in 1998.[24] Americans are more likely to have a great deal of confidence in religious organizations (23.6%) and higher education (18.3%), but even these institutions have declining public support in America.[25]

The American public's disenchantment with government and the political process has clearly been accompanied by a decline in citizens' sense of political efficacy. The u.s. National Election Studies project, which conducts national surveys of the American electorate on a regular basis, has calculated an "External Political Efficacy Index" since 1952.[26] During the fifty-year history of the National Election Studies, the External Political Efficacy Index has declined from an aggregate score of 66 in 1952 to 42 in 1998. Many of the questions used to calculate this index were used in our own survey of Portuguese-Americans in Southeastern Massachusetts to allow comparisons with national findings.

Portuguese-Americans and the Economy

In 1999 and 2000, when our surveys were being conducted, the United States was reaching the peak of one of the most sustained periods of economic growth and prosperity in the last century. The most recent economic expansion was approaching its tenth year, which also made it one of the longest u.s. economic expansions since the end of the Great Depression. Total u.s. employment increased from 108.9 million in 1990 (1ˢᵗQ) to 130.4 million in 2000 (1ˢᵗQ), while the u.s. unemployment rate fell from an annual average of 7.5 percent in 1992 to 4.0 percent in June of 2000. This was not only the lowest unemployment level in 30 years, but it meant the nation had temporarily achieved full employment.[27] During the latter 1990s, productivity (output per worker) also increased at a rate of 3.0 percent annually compared to only 0.9 percent between 1973 and 1992.[28] These developments combined to reverse two decades of declining real family income for the majority of u.s. families as real incomes and hourly wages began to increase again for many Americans for the first time since the mid-1970s.[29]

Massachusetts was also experiencing a period of substantial economic growth. Total employment in the state increased by 3.4 percent from 1990 to 1999. The unemployment rate decreased from 5.5 percent in 1990 to 2.4 percent in August of 2000, compared to a national average of 4.1 percent in the same month. Average annual wages increased in Massachusetts by 16.9 percent from $32,322 in 1995 to $37,787 in 1998.

However, many Americans, especially those employed in low-skill and low-paying jobs did not share in the strong economy and, as a result, questions about economic justice and income distribution are again being raised as a public policy issue.[30] At the same time, the United States generally, but especially Massachusetts, has been shifting from an industrial to a post-industrial economy anchored by information-, service-, and technology-based enterprises.[31] A prerequisite to participating in this "new economy" is that employers increasingly require workers with higher levels of formal education or specialized job skills. This development is potentially troubling in a state where Portuguese-Americans continue to have lower than average levels of formal educational attainment.

On a national basis, a "skills gap" in the new economy was first identified in 1987 by the Hudson Institute's *Workforce 2000* report, which was subsequently reaffirmed in projections by the u.s. Department of Labor, private foundations, and various think-tanks.[32] These sources all projected that by the year 2000, nearly two-thirds of the new jobs created in the United States would require some level of post-secondary

17

education. Approximately one-third of the new jobs were expected to require at least a baccalaureate degree, while another one-third were expected to require a two-year associate's degree or certification by a technical-vocational institute.[33] With an economy based on financial services, business and professional services, and high-tech manufacturing, Massachusetts has become the archetype of a post-industrial economy. Indeed, consistent with earlier projections, the 2000 U.S. Census reports that 33.2 percent of Massachusetts residents now have a bachelor's degree or higher, while 84 percent have at least a high school diploma. On the other hand, formal educational attainment in the Greater New Bedford and Fall River areas remains far behind that of the state as a whole, and current high school drop-out rates do not bode well for the future. A disproportionate amount of this low educational attainment is concentrated among Portuguese-Americans residing in urban ethnic enclaves.

There is reason to be concerned about the lack of formal educational attainment among Portuguese-Americans in Southeastern Massachusetts, since the correlation between incomes and formal education has been growing stronger in the United States over the last two decades.[34] In 1980, the average college graduate in the United States earned approximately thirty percent (30%) more than a high school graduate. By 1993, the "wage premium" attached to a college degree had more than doubled, with the average college graduate now earning seventy percent (70%) more than a high school graduate. Similarly, the average high school graduate earns seventy percent (70%) percent more than a person with a 9th grade education, which in 1990 was the median educational attainment level of New Bedford and Fall River residents –the two Southeastern Massachusetts cities with the largest concentrations of Portuguese-Americans.[35]

Southeastern Massachusetts as whole, but the region's Portuguese-American residents in particular, are characterized by income, employment, and educational levels that lag behind Massachusetts and United States averages by considerable margins. This is especially true of the area's urban centers – Fall River, New Bedford, and Taunton – although many of its rural and suburban towns have educational attainment levels that are also well below state averages. For example, 39.0 percent of Southeastern Massachusetts residents did not have a high school diploma in 1990 compared to 20.0 percent statewide. Similarly, in 1990, only 13.7 percent of the region's residents had a bachelor's degree or higher compared to 27.2 percent statewide. Per capita income in Southeastern Massachusetts was only $13,131 (1990) compared to a statewide average of $17,224, while median household income was $29,920 or 23.5 percent less than the statewide average of $36,952.

While the unemployment rate in Southeastern Massachusetts reached an all-time low of 3.7 percent in August of 2000, this compared to a statewide average of only 2.4 percent. Furthermore, the most significant employment growth in Southeastern Massachusetts has occurred in low-wage retail and services industries, while the area's high-paying manufacturing jobs continue to disappear. These factors lead to the hypothesis that residents of Southeastern Massachusetts have reasons not to be as satisfied with the economy as citizens nationally. This may especially be the case among Portuguese-Americans, since they generally possess lower levels of educational attainment and therefore are more likely to have low-wage jobs and to be more susceptible to unemployment.

Portuguese-Americans on Social and Cultural Issues

Americans are divided into a number of different racial, ethnic, religious, political, and socio-economic groups. In many cases, these groups hold particular and differing attitudes on a range of social and cultural issues. For example, individuals with lower levels of education and lower incomes are less likely to believe that women should have an equal role with men in business, industry, and government than are individuals with higher levels of education and higher incomes. Individuals with a lower socio-economic status are also less likely to support abortion rights and more likely to support prayer in public schools.[36] Differences in social and cultural attitudes are likewise correlated with other demographic characteristics such as occupation, party identity, race, and religion.

The Portuguese-Americans in Southeastern Massachusetts are more recent immigrants to the region than many other groups such as the Irish, French-Canadians, and Polish. In general, Portuguese-Americans have lower levels of education, lower incomes, and are more likely to be employed in unskilled occupations when compared to the region's residents as a whole. Portuguese-Americans are overwhelmingly Catholic, although this is true of most Massachusetts residents, including the large numbers of French-, Irish-, Italian-, Polish-, and Latin-Americans in the state. Thus, it is reasonable to expect that Portuguese-Americans in Southeastern Massachusetts may have distinctive attitudes on various social and cultural issues, including immigration, education, abortion, homosexual unions, and school prayer.

Many of the questions included in our survey of these issues are taken from the General Social Survey (GSS), which is a survey of U.S. households conducted every two years by the National Opinion Research Center (NORC) at the University of Chicago. Some questions were adapted from surveys by other national organizations, including the National Election Studies (NES) conducted by the Center for Political Studies at the University of Michigan, and polls by The Gallop Organization. These national polling organizations have noted significant changes in the social attitudes of respondents during the years that their studies have been conducted in the United States.

For example, the General Social Survey has noted a dramatic increase over the past thirty years in support for racial equality and integration, equal roles for women, the separation of religion from public school, and a steady increase in support for the protection of civil liberties. However, the opinions of Americans have changed very little over the years with regard to many other social issues. Nearly the same percentage of Americans in 1953 (68%) and 2000 (66%) favor the death penalty for a person convicted of murder. Only 19.0 percent of Americans surveyed in both 1975 and 2000 agree that abortions should be illegal under any circumstances. The percentage of survey respondents (41%) in 2000 who agree that immigration should be kept at its present level is just slightly higher than the percentage of respondents who agreed in 1965 (39%) that immigration should be kept at its present level.[37] These national trends are used as benchmarks for comparing the social and cultural attitudes of Portuguese-Americans in Southeastern Massachusetts.

Portuguese Language Instruction

The Center for Policy Analysis also conducted a survey of foreign language instruction in selected communities of the Commonwealth of Massachusetts and in the colleges and universities of Massachusetts. This essay may seem far removed from the other essays, which focus on political, cultural, social, and economic attitudes, but with the decline of Portuguese immigration to Southeastern Massachusetts, it is an important measure of how and whether the region's Portuguese culture and identity will remain vibrant a generation from now. Specifically, the purpose of this study was to determine the extent to which Portuguese language instruction is offered in middle schools and high schools located in towns and cities with significant concentrations of Portuguese-Americans, and whether heritage speakers of Portuguese, as well as English-speaking students, have the opportunity to develop Portuguese language skills in the classroom.

Portuguese is the third most spoken European language and the sixth most spoken language in the world. The Portuguese-speaking world is comprised of approximately 200 million people in seven countries, in three continents, and the many Lusophone communities in the United States and throughout the world. Portuguese is also the language of the second largest city in the world, namely São Paulo, with an estimated population of 16 million. Countries whose official language is Portuguese are Angola, Brazil, Cape Verde, Guinea-Bissau, Mozambique, Portugal, and São Tome e Principe.[38] Brazil is the world's fifth largest country in terms of population and it has the eighth largest economy in the world in terms of gross national product. Brazil's economy is larger than those of all other South American countries and it accounts for 36 percent of Latin America's GDP, which is more than Mexico (26%), Argentina (8%), and Chile (4%). The Brazilian economy has continuously outpaced the GDP growth rate of Latin America as a whole since 1993.[39]

Furthermore, the language, literatures and cultures of the Portuguese-speaking world are experiencing an increase in visibility and interest, which is confirmed by the Nobel Prize for Literature awarded to José Saramago in 1998. In short, the significant numbers of Portuguese-speaking persons throughout the world, coupled with the increasing recognition of the cultures of the Portuguese-speaking world, demonstrates a significant reason for offering Portuguese language instruction in Massachusetts public schools.

However, there are also very practical reasons for increasing Portuguese language instruction in Massachusetts public schools, colleges, and universities that are recognized in state and national education policy statements. In 1989, at a national education summit, President of the United States George H. Bush, the u.s. Secretary of Education William Bennett, and the governors of the 50 states agreed to establish measurable goals for education reform that were embodied in a report called *America 2000*. Building on this momentum, in 1990, u.s. Secretary of Labor, Lynn Martin charged the Secretary's Commission on Achieving Necessary Skills with the task of specifying the skills required for success in the new economy. The SCAN's report concludes that in order "to encourage a high-performance economy characterized by high-skills, high-wage employment" school, college, and university curricula must emphasize skills such as math, research, and communications, including foreign language instruction.[40]

On June 18, 1993, Massachusetts Governor William Weld signed the Massachusetts Education Reform Act, a comprehensive and ambitious education improvement initiative consistent with the *America 2000* national education objectives. This act recognizes the importance of teaching students proficiency in a second language to enable them to participate as workers in a multilingual global economy and as citizens in a world without borders. The Massachusetts Education Reform Act suggests that a knowledge of other languages and cultures will enhance workers' communicative proficiency, will aid in cross-cultural communication, and will allow them to obtain information directly from other countries where access would be limited. The Act also recognizes the importance of establishing a link between local and global communities by drawing upon the strong ethnic and linguistic heritage of various Massachusetts towns and cities.

Over the last two decades, this goal has become increasingly urgent because economic globalization has transformed the international business environment. The term *globalization* is widely used to encompass a variety of unprecedented technological, economic, cultural, social, and political trends that are extending the boundaries of the world's social systems beyond the borders of nation-states.[41] International education and career opportunities are opening for bilingual or multi-lingual workers in the fields of foreign affairs, trade and finance, tourism, publishing and broadcasting, cultural institutions and foundations, scientific research and development, and higher education.

Globalization is perhaps most pronounced in economic relations, which are now characterized by global competition, the emergence of globally integrated transnational enterprises (TNEs), and advances in information technology, transportation, and multilateral trade arrangements. Major competitors of the United States economy have emerged in Asia and Europe and are emerging in parts of Latin America. This means that United States education policy must not only cultivate more educated workers, it must cultivate workers and citizens with multinational competencies. In this respect, a 1983 report by the National Commission on Excellence in Education was one of the earliest to recognize that the study of a foreign language serves the nation's needs in commerce, diplomacy, defense and education.[42]

Such observations are more true today than they were two decades ago. In recent years, as national boundaries have become porous to immigration, capital flows, and commodities trade, cities and regions have displaced nations as the focus of international economic competition. Regional or metropolitan clusters of internationally competitive industries have tended to replace trade barriers, subsidies, and other national protections as the basis of economic development.[43] For instance, in Southeastern Massachusetts, textiles and apparel, electronics manufacturing, aquaculture and marine technology are important clusters, where the region has established an international presence. With more than one-third of the region's population of Portuguese ancestry, the Portuguese ethnic presence gives the regional economy a direct connection to important segments of the global economy, including the European Union, Latin America, and Asia.

Findings and Conclusions

In conducting the surveys assembled in this book, every effort was made to insure the methodological validity of the findings (see Appendix A), but as with all forays into new areas of inquiry, it is risky to make bold generalizations about Portuguese-Americans. The purpose of the studies was not to provide a definitive answer to the question, "Who are the Portuguese?" The purpose was to stimulate discussion among

Portuguese-Americans about their political future and to catalyze inter-est among social scientists in the study of Portuguese-American political behavior and ethnic identity. This process began with a one-day confer-ence held at the University of Massachusetts Dartmouth on October 28, 2000, which was sponsored by the UMD Center for Portuguese Studies and Culture and the Luso-American Foundation. The conference was convened for the purpose of discussing the preliminary findings of these studies. It was attended by more than 100 persons, including university faculty, Massachusetts state legislators, labor union officials, journalists, community activists, and the general public. The conference received extensive local press coverage in both the English and Portuguese lan-guage press.[44] It is hoped that the publication of this book will extend that discussion to a national and international audience, while making an inroad into the academic enclaves of ethnic studies, political science, and sociology.

So who are the Portuguese in Southeastern Massachusetts? The final essay in this collection compares the 1999-2000 research findings with an earlier study, *Luso-Americans in the American Political Process* (1992), that was prepared in 1977 by Dr. Rita Marinho. Dr. Marinho's chapter makes some basic comparisons of how Portuguese-Americans in Southeastern Massachusetts have changed during the last 25 years, while pointing to several factors that have remained constant during this time. There are always exceptions to every generalization, but on the whole Portuguese-Americans in Southeastern Massachusetts have disturbingly low levels of formal educational attainment when compared to the U.S. and Massachusetts population. They occupy predominantly blue-collar occupations, but like other Americans they have low levels of union membership. The Portuguese remain overwhelmingly Catholic, although the Catholic Church seems to exert very little influence on political behavior and does not constitute a significant source of politi-cal information for Portuguese-Americans. As with most residents in Massachusetts, the Portuguese are heavily Democratic in their political party identification and yet, as discussed later, there is an identifiable tension between the "Portuguese ideology" and the current policy direc-tion of the Democratic party.

In many ways, Portuguese-Americans exemplify the model minority in the United States. The Portuguese arrived in the United States with little education and few skills but became a mainstay of the fishing and manufacturing industries in Southeastern Massachusetts.[45] They have a strong work ethic and believe that a good education and working hard are the keys to personal economic success. A higher than average percentage of Portuguese-Americans still work in blue-collar jobs that require low levels of educational attainment, and these jobs provide lower than average incomes. Nevertheless, they are generally satisfied with their economic progress over the last five years, have a better standard of living than that of their parents, and they are optimistic about the prospects of their children to be better off than themselves. A large majority of the region's Portuguese-Americans are satisfied with their jobs and, in a strong economy, there appears to be little concern about the prospect of unemployment. Despite a massive wave of deindustrialization that swept the region less than a decade earlier, Portuguese-Americans seem to have adapted with a great deal of resilience and have shown the ability to adapt quickly to changing economic conditions, particularly in their increased recognition of the importance of education in the new economy.[46]

However, all is not well among the Portuguese of Southeastern Massachusetts. Portuguese-Americans certainly recognize that pockets of poverty and unemployment still exist in the region and that public schools will have to be improved to insure the optimistic expectations they have about their children. Hence, our survey findings reveal that Portuguese-Americans are concerned about the nation's lack of progress in reducing poverty, express doubts about the quality of public education, and consider it government's responsibility to insure economic equity. Moreover, these anxieties are not abstract concerns for many of the Portuguese in Southeastern Massachusetts.

The sample size is not sufficient to make a definitive claim, but the Taunton survey found that about 13 percent of Portuguese respondents were unemployed at a time when state and local unemployment rates were less than 4 percent. The Center's survey did not measure "unemployment" using the official u.s. Bureau of Labor Statistics definition, but simply asked whether a person was employed (including as a homemaker). The large number of unemployed, using our broader definition, suggests that many Portuguese-Americans may be chronically unemployed (and perhaps unemployable with current skills) and, for that reason, they simply do not register in official statistics.[47]

Moreover, while Portuguese-Americans in Southeastern Massachusetts report that they are generally satisfied with their job security and the physical safety of their workplaces, nearly half (46.7%) are not satisfied with their chance for promotion. This concern could be an effect of their low educational attainment, their concentration in declining and downsizing industries, or subtle forms of ethnic discrimination. While a large majority of Portuguese-Americans, like other Americans, are satisfied with their health care benefits, approximately one-third (32.8%) are not satisfied with those benefits and more than a third (36.7%) are not satisfied with their current medical and family leave benefits. Similarly, nearly one-third (30.0%) are dissatisfied with their current pension benefits. Although a majority of the region's Portuguese-Americans are satisfied with their current earnings, more than a third (36.4%) are dissatisfied with their earnings.

Thus, there is a significant pocket of discontent among Portuguese-Americans that largely consists of persons holding low-wage jobs and having low levels of educational attainment. This pocket of discontent also consists disproportionately of persons who are foreign-born, and since many of these persons are not U.S. citizens, they are not eligible to vote. Therefore, the political alienation of this disaffected group of Portuguese-Americans is not likely to register in normal electoral politics. These are the very people who are least likely to vote, the least likely to belong to political or civic organizations, the least likely to contact government officials, and the least likely to be politically informed at even the most basic level.

This is a significant finding since our surveys also indicate that when the Portuguese become U.S. citizens *and register to vote,* they tend to vote in high proportions, although like most Americans they have low levels of basic political information. For example, one-third of the respondents in the Taunton survey could not name the mayor of Taunton or the governor of Massachusetts, and these findings were replicated in a second survey of the entire Archipelago. These low levels of political information are strongly correlated with low levels of educational attainment and lower incomes, which leads to the intriguing hypothesis that these respondents may be the same group of Portuguese-Americans that have low levels of political efficacy and who express dissatisfaction with their current economic conditions.[48]

Moreover, despite recognizing the importance of education to economic success, their overall satisfaction with the quality of public schools suggests continuing difficulty in adjusting to a constantly rising performance bar in the United States. Southeastern Massachusetts has some of the poorest performing schools in the Commonwealth of Massachusetts as measured by chronic absenteeism, high school drop-out rates, standardized test scores, and rates of college attendance.[49] It is quite notable that persons with lower levels of educational attainment are more likely to be dissatisfied with the quality of public schools.

It appears that Portuguese-Americans in Southeastern Massachusetts are a hybrid variant of what Verba and Nie call "the voter specialist." Voter specialists are political participants who confine their political activism to regularized voting and occasional efforts to persuade others how to vote. Portuguese-Americans are hybrid voter specialists insofar as their voting behavior (and other forms of political participation) are more intently focused on local elections, where they have neighborhood enclaves, access to Portuguese-language media, and a greater probability of finding Portuguese candidates running for office. The Portuguese clearly express a stronger attachment to local politics than to national politics, despite the fact that issues such as immigration reform, deportation, and East Timor directly affect large numbers of Portuguese-Americans in Southeastern Massachusetts. However, it is not clear whether their greater attachment to local politics is peculiar to the Portuguese in Southeastern Massachusetts and perhaps related to the number of Portuguese-Americans holding public office as state legislators, mayors, city councilors, and town selectmen.

Portuguese-Americans who are registered to vote turn out to vote in comparatively high proportions for all types elections, but they are also hybrid voter specialists in the sense that they are more likely to make particularized contacts with government officials than most Americans, particularly with local government officials. Portuguese-Americans also express their greatest sense of political efficacy at the local level. Thus, it is most interesting that Portuguese-Americans are much more likely to make particularized or parochial contacts with government officials than the average American, but the vast majority feel they need an intermediary or political connection to help them make contact. This finding suggests that Portuguese-Americans who are elected to office provide an important conduit between Portuguese-Americans and government. This also suggests the need for strong civic and political associations in the Portuguese community to facilitate these contacts on a wider basis.

The idea that strong civic associations make a difference to political participation and political efficacy is supported by other evidence. Aside from the small number of persons who are simply "not interested in politics," the vast majority (85.7%) of Portuguese-Americans who are U.S. citizens, but not registered to vote, state that they are interested in registering if the opportunity is made easily available, if someone would show them how to register, and if literacy assistance is available to help them fill out the registration form where language is a problem. This suggests that even among Portuguese-Americans who are already U.S. citizens, a fertile ground exists for voter registration campaigns, particularly if these campaigns are tied to local electoral races involving Portuguese-American candidates. Given their stronger attachments to local government, these campaigns are likely to be most successful when organized around races for the state legislature, city council, mayor, school committee, and similar elections.

Our findings also indicate that the more salient differences in occupation, income, and education are between foreign-born and U.S.-born Portuguese than between U.S.-born Portuguese and other Americans. This finding suggests that the Portuguese integrate into the U.S. economy and become involved in local politics by the second or third generation, even while maintaining a distinct culture and a living language within ethnic neighborhoods, sports clubs, and fraternal societies. Significantly, when the Center's surveys are compared to earlier studies of the Portuguese in Southeastern Massachusetts, it is clear that membership in Portuguese political organizations has been decreasing over the last 25 years, while membership in various civic associations, particularly sports clubs and social clubs, has been increasing over the same period. One inference from this finding is that in contrast to many other U.S. ethnic or racial groups (e.g., African-Americans or Mexican-Americans), Portuguese ethnic identity is becoming a predominantly social or cultural identity and not a political one.[50]

This conclusion is further supported by our finding that a majority of Portuguese-Americans in Southeastern Massachusetts do not think it is necessary for a person to be a member of a particular ethnic group to represent that group's interests. Only 20 percent of the Portuguese-Americans surveyed felt strongly that being of the same ethnicity made a difference in an elected official's ability to represent a particular ethnic group. This may be an increase from the 6 percent reported in Marinho's 1977 study, but it is difficult to tell whether this is a real increase or merely the effect of slightly different questions. Regardless of how this methodological question gets resolved in the future, our findings also reveal that 73 percent of the Portuguese-Americans surveyed believe that they are well represented in important government and business institutions in Southeastern Massachusetts.

However, the findings on Portuguese ethnic identity are far from unequivocal. There are many statistically significant differences between the responses of Portuguese and non-Portuguese respondents on questions related to ethnic identity. Portuguese respondents are more likely to think of themselves as members of a particular ethnic, racial, or nationality group than are non-Portuguese respondents. They are also more likely to have felt discrimination because of their ethnicity, with nearly a third (32.0%) of Portuguese-Americans reporting they have felt discrimination because of their ethnicity or race. Yet Portuguese-Americans are about evenly divided over whether applying to the federal government for official "minority" status would create educational and job opportunities that are better, the same, or worse than those for non-minority groups.

At the same time, a higher percentage of Portuguese respondents feel that racial and ethnic groups should maintain their distinct cultures as compared to non-Portuguese respondents. A majority of Portuguese respondents feel that racial and ethnic groups should maintain their distinct cultures (52.7%) in comparison to non-Portuguese respondents (31.2%). This feeling is particularly strong among foreign-born Portuguese (70.3%) as compared to Portuguese who were born in the United States (44.6%). Yet a large majority of Portuguese-Americans say they think of themselves as "just an American," even though a higher percentage of Portuguese respondents consider themselves members of a particular ethnic, racial, or nationality group (24.6%) than non-Portuguese respondents (3.2%). Notably, Portuguese respondents who were not born in the United States are far more likely to think of themselves as a member of a particular ethnic, racial, or nationality group (50.0%) than Portuguese respondents who were born in the United States (12.7%), which suggests that a certain degree of assimilation is occurring in subsequent generations.

In this respect, the Portuguese are like many u.s. immigrant groups who have embraced a "melting pot" concept of identity, which does not put their sense of being "Portuguese" in conflict with being "American." The characteristics identified by Portuguese as most important to being an American, in order of importance, are u.s. citizenship, the ability to speak English, and being born in the United States. This concept of being "American" explains why a large number of Portuguese-Americans –particularly, the foreign-born, those without u.s. citizenship, and those who speak English poorly – may continue to feel marginalized in their adopted country and have a stronger sense of Portuguese identity. While a foreign-born individual may learn English and obtain u.s. citizenship, it is only their children – born in the United States – who are perceived as "truly" and "completely" American even within the Portuguese-American community.

Consistent with this finding is the fact that a surprisingly large majority of both Portuguese and non-Portuguese respondents favor a law making English the official language of the United States. It is certainly true that Portuguese respondents are more likely than non-Portuguese respondents to oppose a law making English the official language of the United States, but foreign-born Portuguese are the only group in our sample to strongly oppose the adoption of an "English-only" law. Similarly, while all groups agree that rates of immigration to the United States should remain the same or decrease, the only significant pocket of support for increased immigration was among foreign-born Portuguese-Americans.

In this respect, the Portuguese-American community is deeply fractured between a significant minority who feel that Portuguese ethnicity should be constituted as a political identity, versus the substantial majority who view Portuguese ethnicity as primarily a social and cultural identity. The significant minority currently finds its strongest base of support among the foreign-born Portuguese, and this is the same group that is most likely to feel that they do not get enough attention from government. Of course, due to statutory barriers such as non-citizenship, language barriers, and education, this is the very segment of the Portuguese community that is least likely to be politically active in any form. The Portuguese report that they are less "interested in politics" than other groups, and this finding is particularly true of the foreign born, especially if they are not United States citizens. Furthermore, while this group overlaps with those who express discontent about their economic situation, the two groups are distinct enough to raise questions about whether they can combine in sufficient strength to realign Portuguese identity in a political direction.[51]

However, even if Portuguese-Americans were to agree on a distinct political identity, to become citizens in larger numbers, register to vote in larger numbers and therefore vote in larger numbers, what is their potential impact on the regional politics of Southeastern Massachusetts? Independent of whether mobilizing Portuguese-Americans would lead to the election of more Portuguese-American candidates, there are some potentially significant impacts. For instance, at a time when party identification, particularly among Democrats, has been weakening at both the state and national levels, Portuguese-Americans remain staunchly loyal to the Democratic party and the principles of economic liberalism.[52] Nearly all of the region's Portuguese-Americans who voted in the 1996 u.s. Presidential election voted for Bill Clinton. This is a landslide majority that is unmatched by any other ethnic group with the exception of African-Americans. It is a particularly striking majority when compared to other white Caucasian voters in the United States, including blue-collar workers, whose support for Democratic candidates is much weaker than that reported by Portuguese-Americans with the same demographic characteristics.

Yet, Portuguese-American support for the Democratic party cannot be taken for granted because it is clear that a psychological and ideological disjuncture is emerging between them. Despite their stated preference for the Democratic party, Portuguese-Americans' psychological attachment to the Democratic party appears to be weakening, which is consistent with a long-term statewide and national trend of declining party identification and "split ticket" voting.[53] Indeed, even while expressing strong support for the Democratic party, about 60 percent of Portuguese-Americans dismissed party affiliation as important to a candidate's ability to represent their interests.

This finding is particularly interesting as the Democratic party continues it move toward a "neo-liberal" mix of fiscal conservatism and cultural liberalism in response to national trends in voter behavior. The Portuguese-Americans responding to our surveys reveal a peculiar mix of liberal and conservative views that stands in sharp contrast to the "changing American voter." There have been two dominant trends in the American electorate over the last two decades with respect to party affiliation and ideological orientation. The number of persons who consider themselves Independents, rather than identifying with either major party, has increased consistently since the early 1970s, so that more persons now identify themselves as Independent than identify with either of the two major political parties.[54] The rising number of Independents has been accompanied by a shift in ideological orientation, where more and more voters, especially middle class educated voters, have adopted an ideological orientation that is economically and fiscally conservative and socially and culturally liberal. This perspective has certainly characterized electoral outcomes in Massachusetts during the last decade.

Portuguese-Americans appear to be headed in the opposite direction. In general, Portuguese-Americans articulate a hybrid ideology that is best described as economically liberal, socially liberal (i.e., individual and group rights), but culturally conservative (i.e., moral values). As mentioned earlier, the survey of economic opinion and rates of economic satisfaction reveals that most Portuguese-Americans are optimistic about their economic situation, but are disturbed by the lack of progress on reducing poverty, and they strongly agree that inequalities of wealth and income are too wide in the United States. Moreover, Portuguese-Americans consider it government's responsibility to address these issues in the economy. Portuguese-Americans in Southeastern Massachusetts were also surprisingly liberal, given the conventional wisdom, on a variety of social issues involving individual and group rights, such as support for bilingual education, the recognition of gender inequities in employment, opposition to the death penalty, conditional support of abortion rights, and tolerance of homosexual unions. However, u.s.-born Portuguese were significantly more liberal on these social issues than foreign-born Portuguese.

At the same time, Portuguese-Americans express opinions on a vari-

ety of other issues that would ordinarily be described as culturally conservative, such as the belief that ethnic groups should assimilate into the
"mainstream" of American society, support for prayer in public schools,
support for public funding of parochial schools, a belief that becoming
an "American" means becoming a u.s. citizen, speaking English, and living in the United States for most of one's life, support for the deportation of legal aliens convicted of felony crimes, and concern about exposing children to violence in movies and on television. Furthermore, most
Portuguese-Americans in Southeastern Massachusetts report that they
do not feel discriminated against because of their ethnicity. Yet, on
many of these issues, it is the foreign-born Portuguese who anchor the
conservative tendency, with many u.s.-born Portuguese adopting liberal
views on most (but not all) cultural issues in the same proportions as
Americans generally.[55]

33

However, any potential impact on regional or statewide politics
depends on the ability of Portuguese-Americans to enter the political
system in greater numbers and to do so as a coherent political force with
a unified voice. As noted earlier, Portuguese-Americans vote and register
to vote in about the same proportions as other u.s. citizens, but of
course large numbers of Portuguese-Americans cannot register to vote
because they are not u.s. citizens. Thus, in addition to the usual problems of constructing a coherent political identity, targeting issues
important to the Portuguese-American community, and mobilizing voters during elections, those interested in Portuguese-American political
participation face the added burden of promoting citizenship among
their cohorts. There are many ethnic legends about why so many
Portuguese fail to become citizens, but the survey evidence does not
support these claims in Southeastern Massachusetts. Quite the contrary,
a vast majority of the Portuguese interviewed for these studies express a
desire to become u.s. citizens, but they simply do not know how to do
so or even know how to initiate an application. The problem is not
determined by "culture." It is a problem of political information and
immigrant assistance.

The survey findings also argue for building the social capital of the
Portuguese community generally. While many of the findings in this
book replicate the expectations of the standard socio-economic model
of political behavior, the surveys also found that persons who belong to

political organizations, civic associations, as well as those who read newspapers, are more likely to register to vote, more likely to vote, more likely to try to influence the voting of others, and likely to have a greater sense of political efficacy. Thus, while sports clubs, fraternal organizations, and Portuguese language media outlets may all be non-partisan or even non-political on their surface, they provide a cultural support mechanism and an institutional training ground for political activity and political leadership. A high percentage of Portuguese-Americans in Taunton report that they still obtain political information from Portuguese language media outlets, and our findings indicate that the Portuguese have greater levels of trust and confidence in the mass media than other groups in the region.

Finally, one question that emerged from the October 28, 2000 conference is whether there is a distinct Portuguese-American interest in state and national politics? It is certain that neither our preliminary research, nor the subsequent conference, can fully answer that question, but we are prepared to draw some rudimentary conclusions. The Portuguese-American interest in the U.S. political process derives from a combination of historical, cultural, and socio-economic factors. The historical and cultural factors largely define a "foreign policy" interest that includes immigration issues, deportation, cultural exchange, Portuguese language instruction in U.S. public schools, and greater involvement in East Timor. Any progress on these issues will require the combined foreign policy efforts of Lusophone governments with domestic lobbying from Portuguese-American political groups, because these issues do not command great support from most non-Portuguese voters. The Portuguese-Americans' socio-economic status, in Southeastern Massachusetts at least, largely defines a "domestic policy" interest that includes access to improved education and higher education, workforce development and worker displacement assistance, worker rights, better wages, medical benefits, pension benefits, and a whole range of other issues that affect blue-collar workers in the new economy. These two sets of issues merge for Portuguese-Americans in the process of economic globalization and trade liberalization, which is having a profound impact on the low-skilled manufacturing jobs in Southeastern Massachusetts that have been the mainstay of Portuguese-American well-being for more than a century. In a word, Portuguese-Americans in Southeastern

Massachusetts, more than many other groups, are faced simultaneously with the problems of adjusting to economic globalization, deindustrialization, and the meaning of citizenship in a new country.

Notes

[1]U.S. Census Bureau, *Census of Population and Housing, 1990*. At the time of publication, the 2000 data for ancestry, educational attainment, and income had not been released by the U.S. Census Bureau and it was not scheduled to be released for several months.

[2]Ancestry refers to a person's ethnic origin or descent, cultural heritage, or the place of birth of the person or that of the person's parents or ancestors before they arrived in the United States. In the U.S. Census, the term "single ancestry" includes persons who report only one ethnic group. The term "first ancestry" includes persons who report only Portuguese and also those who report Portuguese first and then some other group. The term "secondary ancestry" includes persons who report Portuguese second and some other group first (1990 U.S. *Census of Population and Housing*).

[3]Other significant concentrations of Portuguese-Americans are found in Gloucester and Chicopee, Massachusetts. Historically, Gloucester is an important participant in the state's fishing industry, while Chicopee was a major center of the textile industry.

[4]Jose Luis Ribeiro, *Portuguese Immigrants and Education* (Bristol, RI: Portuguese-American Federation, 1982); Jerry Williams, *And Yet They Come: Portuguese Immigration from the Azores to the United States* (Staten Island, NY: Center for Migration Studies, 1982); John Silva, Jr., *Azoreans in America and Americans in the Azores* (Bristol, RI: Portuguese-American Federation, 1969). U.S. immigration data only identifies individuals as "Portuguese" if they emigrated from Portugal or its islands. It is known that many Portuguese-speaking people emigrate from countries other than Portugal (e.g. Brazil, Canada, France, Angola, Mozambique) and, consequently, the number of Lusophone immigrants is likely higher than the official numbers.

[5]Following an earthquake in 1957, Senator John F. Kennedy introduced special legislation that authorized additional immigration from the island of Faial, which helped facilitate the third wave of Azorean immigration to the United States.

[6]Everett S. Allen, *Children of the Light: The Rise and Fall of New Bedford Whaling and the Death of the Arctic Fleet* (Boston: Little, Brown, and Co., 1973).

[7]Williams, *And Yet They Come*.

[8]Aluisio Medeiros da Rosa Borges. 1990. *The Portuguese Working Class in the Durfee Mills of Fall River, Massachusetts* (Binghamton: State University of New York, Ph.D. Dissertation, 1990); Philip T. Silvia, Jr., *The Spindle City: Labor, Politics, and Religion in Fall River, 1870-185*, 2 Vols. (New York: P.T. Silvia, 1973).

[9]See, Ribeiro, *Portuguese Immigrants and Education*.

[10]Curriculum Research and Development Center, *The Need to Develop a System for the Assessment/Testing of Portuguese Speaking Students* (Kingston, RI: University of Rhode Island, 1997).

[11]Gary Gerstle, *The American Crucible: Race and Nation in the Twentieth Century* (Princeton: Princeton University Press, 2001); Lawrence Fuchs, *The American Kaleidoscope: Ethnicity and the Civic Culture* (Hanover, NH: University Press of New England, 1991); Harry A. Bailey, and Ellis Katz, *Ethnic Group Politics* (Columbus, OH: Merrill and Co., 1969); Edgar Litt, *Ethnic Politics in America: Beyond Pluralism* (Glenview, IL: Scott Foresman, 1970); Susan Olzak and Joane Nagel, eds., *Competitive Ethnic Relations* (Orlando: Academic Press, 1986); Hanes Walton, Jr., *African American Power and Politics: The Political Context Variable* (New York: Columbia University Press, 1997); Angela T. Pienkos, ed., *Ethnic Politics in Urban America: The Polish Experience in Four Cities* (Chicago: Polish American Historical Association, 1978); Edward R. Kantowicz, *Polish-American Politics in Chicago, 1888-1940* (Chicago: University of Chicago Press, 1975); Steven Erie, *Rainbow's End: Irish Americans and the Dilemmas of Urban Machine Politics* (Berkeley and Los Angeles, University of California Press, 1990); Philip A. Bean, "The Irish, the Italians, and Machine Politics, A Case Study: Utica, New York (1870-1960)," *Journal of Urban History* 20 (1994): 205-39; Juan Gonzalez, *Harvest of Empire: A History of Latinos in America* (New York: Penguin, 2001); Roberto Suro, *Strangers Among Us: How Latino Immigration is Transforming America* (New York: Alfred A. Knopf, 1998); Jorge Chapa, "Mexican-American Class Structure and Political Participation," *New*

England Journal of Public Policy, Vol. 2, No. 1 (Spring/Summer 1995): 183-98; Jose Cruz, "Puerto Rican Politics in the United States: A Preliminary Assessment," *New England Journal of Public Policy,* Vol. 2, No. 1 (Spring/Summer 1995): 199-219; Helen Zia, *Asian-American Dreams: The Emergence of an American People* (New York: Farrar, Straus, and Giroux, 2000); Karin Aguilar San Juan, ed., *The State of Asian America: Activism and Resistance in the 1990s* (Boston: South End Press, 1994).

[12]Rita Duarte Marinho, *Os Luso-Americanos No Porcesso Politico Americano Estudo Duma Situacao Concreta* (Angra do Heroismo: Gabinete de Emigração e Apoio as Comunidades Açorianas, 1992); Leo Pap, *The Portuguese-Americans* (Boston: Twayne, 1981).

[13]Toby E. Huff, "Education and Ethnicity in Southeastern Massachusetts," *New England Board of Higher Education: Issues in Planning and Policymaking* (Boston: New England Board of Higher Education, 1989), pp. 1-8.

[14]Raymond E. Wolfinger and Steven J. Rosenstone, *Who Votes?* (New Haven: Yale University Press, 1980).

[15]A study of civic and political participation among Portuguese-Americans in Taunton, Massachusetts was conducted at the request of the Luso-American Citizenship Project of Taunton. It was funded by the Luso-American Development Foundation.

[16]A series of surveys was conducted by the University of Massachusetts Dartmouth Center for Policy Analysis in 1999 and 2000 in collaboration with the institution's Center for Portuguese Studies and Culture. The surveys were funded by the University of Massachusetts Dartmouth Center for Portuguese Studies and Culture.

[17]Sidney Verba and Norman H. Nie, *Participation in America* (New York: Harper and Row, 1972), p. 2.

[18]Gabriel Almond and Sidney Verba, *The Civic Culture: Political Attitudes and Democracy in Five Nations, an analytic study* (Boston: Little, Brown, and Co., 1965); Gabriel Almond and Sidney Verba, *The Civic Culture Revisited: An Analytic Study* (Boston: Little, Brown, and Co., 1980).

[19]Robert Putnam, *Bowling Alone: The Collapse and Revival of American Community* (New York: Simon and Schuster, 2000), Chaps. 2-8.

[20]Australia, Austria, Belgium, Canada, Denmark, France, Finland, Germany, Greece, Iceland, Ireland, Italy, Japan, Luxemburg, Netherlands, New Zeland, Norway, Spain, Sweden, Switzerland, United Kingdom, United States. See Robert A. Dahl, *Polyarchy: Participation and Opposition* (New Haven: Yale University Press, 1971), pp. 248-49

[21]U.S. Department of Commerce, Bureau of the Census, *Statistical Abstract of the United States* (Washington, D.C.: Government Printing Office, 1999), p. 301.

[22]Center on Policy Attitudes, "Expecting More to Say," in *The American Public On Its Role in Government Decision-Making* (Washington, DC, 1999).

[23]Ibid.

[24]National Election Studies, "Time Series Studies, 1952-1998," (Ann Arbor: University of Michigan, 2000).

[25]U.S. Department of Commerce, Bureau of the Census, *Statistical Abstract of the United States* (Washington, DC: Government Printing Office, 1999), p. 299.

[26]External political efficacy generally refers to the degree to which individuals feels that the political process is responsive to their concerns and needs. Internal political efficacy relates to the level at which individuals actually participate in the political process (e.g. voting, working on campaigns).

[27]Economists define full employment "as the availability of work at prevailing wage rates for all persons who desire it" (Shim and Siegel 1995, 156), which for most economists means an unemployment rate of 4 percent or less. Full employment does not mean 100 percent employment, since there is always some unemployment owing to job changes (frictional unemployment) and seasonal factors (e.g., construction or teaching).

[28]Office of the U.S. President, *Economic Report of the President, 1993* (Washington, DC.: Government Printing Office, 1993), Chap. 1:1.

[29]Lawrence Mishel and Jared Bernstein, *Declining Wages for High School and College Graduates: Pay And Benefits Trends by Education, Gender, Occupation, and State, 1979-1991* (Washington, DC: Economic Policy Institute, 1992); Office of the U.S. President, *Economic Report of the President, 1993.*

[30]Lawrence Mishel, Jared Bernstein, and John Schmitt, *The State of Working America, 1998-1999* (Ithaca, NY: Cornell University Press, 1999); Office of the U.S. President, *Economic Report of the*

President, 1997 (Washington, DC: Government Printing Office, 1997), Chap. 5; Massachusetts AFL-CIO, *Work and Family: Putting People First; Labor's Public Policy Agenda for Massachusetts in 1998 and Beyond* (Boston: Labor Resource Center, University of Massachusetts Boston, 1998).

[31]Daniel Bell, *The Coming of Post-Industrial Society* (New York: Basic Books, 1973); Craig L. Moore and Edward Moscovitch, *The New Economic Reality: Massachusetts Prospects for Long-Term Growth* (Amherst, MA: University of Massachusetts Amherst School of Management, 1994).

[32]William B. Johnston, *Workforce 2000: Work and Workers for the Twenty-First Century* (Indianapolis: Hudson Institute, 1987); G.T. Silvestri and J.M. Lukasiewicz, "Projections 2000: A Look at Occupational Employment Trends to the Year 2000," *Monthly Labor Review*, Vol. 110, No. 9 (September 1987): 46-69; Garth L. Mangum, *Youth and America's Future* (New York: William T. Grant Commission on Work, Family, and Citizenship, 1989).

[33]Commission on the Skills of the American Workforce, *America's Choice: High Skills or Low Wages!* (Rochester, NY: National Center on Education and the Economy, 1990).

[34]National Center for Education Statistics, *The Condition of Education 1989* (Washington, DC: Government Printing Office, 1989); National Center for Education Statistics, *The Condition of Education 1998* (Washington, DC: Government Printing Office, 1998).

[35]U.S. Department of Commerce, Bureau of the Census, *Statistical Abstract of the United States 1999* (Washington, DC: Government Printing Office, 1999), p. 475.

[36]National Election Studies.

[37]Gallup 2000. www.gallup.com/poll/soc_issues.asp

[38]Persons of Cape Verdean and Brazilian heritage are significant components of the Lusophone population in Massachusetts. In the 1990 U.S. Census, persons of Cape Verdean heritage had the option of identifying themselves as Portuguese, African-American, or Other. However, with the existing Census data it is not possible to determine what number of Cape Verdeans are or are not included in the category of Portuguese ancestry. It is also estimated that approximately 15,000 Brazilian-born persons now reside in Massachusetts. See, Andrew Sum and W. Neal Fogg, *The Changing Workforce: Immigrants and the New Economy in Massachusetts* (Boston: Massachusetts Institute for a New Commonwealth, 1999), p. 38.

[39]World Bank, *World Development Report, 1999-2000* (Washington, DC: International Bank for Reconstruction and Development, 2000).

[40]U.S. Department of Labor, *Teaching the SCANS Competencies* (Washington, DC: Secretary's Commission on Achieving Necessary Skills, 1993).

[41]Manfred B. Steger, *Globalism: The New Market Ideology* (Lanham, MD: Rowman and Littlefield Publishers, 2001).

[42]National Commission on Excellence in Education, *A Nation At Risk: The Imperative for Educational Reform* (Washington, DC: U.S. Department of Education, 1983).

[43]Michael Porter, *The Competitive Advantage of Nations* (New York: Free Press, 1990); Michael Porter, *The Competitive Advantage of Massachusetts* (Boston: Secretary of the Commonwealth, 1991).

[44]João Ferreira, "Portuguese-Americans Wield Untapped Power, Study Says," *Sunday New Bedford Standard-Times*, October 22, 2000, pp. C1-C2; João Ferreira, "Portuguese Primed for Progress," *Sunday New Bedford Standard-Times*, October 29, 2000, pp. A1-A4; Marc Munroe Dion, "Seminar Explores Portuguese Issues," *The Fall River Herald News*, October 29, 2000, p. B2; Frank B. Baptista, "Voz do Emigrante: Politics Focus of Study," *The Fall River Sunday Herald News*, January 7, 2001, pp. B1-B2; Frank B. Baptista, "Voz do Emigrante: Study Shows Range of Views," *The Fall River Sunday Herald News*, January 14, 2001, pp. B1-B2; Frank B. Baptista, "Voz do Emigrante," *The Fall River Sunday Herald News*, January 21, 2001, pp. B1-B2; Diana Victor, "UMass Study Looks at Portuguese Voting and Social Views," *O Jornal*, October 25, 2000, pp. 1, 10; Diana Victor, "Afinal, 'quem são os Portugueses?" *O Jornal*, November 1, 2000, pp. 1-2; "Inquerito do Centro de Estudos Portugueses da UMass Dartmouth Revela," *Portuguese Times*, November 9, 2000, p.1.

[45]Rosa P. Rodrigues, *Occupational Mobility of Portuguese Males in New Bedford, Massachusetts, 1870-1900* (New York: New School for Social Research, Ph.D. Dissertation, 1990).

[46]Cf. Dorothy A. Gilbert, *Recent Portuguese Immigrants to Fall River, Massachusetts: An Analysis of Relative Economic Success* (New York: AMS Press, Inc., 1989).

[47]The United States Department of Labor conducts a monthly survey to measure changes in the labor force and unemployment rates. To be counted as "unemployed," a person must not be employed, but must have also actively sought employment during the last 4 weeks. A person who

37

is not actively seeking employment (e.g., discouraged workers) are not counted as part of the official labor force. This "disguised unemployment" simply does not register in the official unemployment statistics (Shim and Siegel 1995, 105-106).

[48]It was not possible to test this hypothesis directly, since the political efficacy, economic satisfaction, and political behavior surveys were conducted separately to prevent the surveys from becoming too long and losing respondents' interest.

[49]David R. Borges and Clyde W. Barrow, *Fall River Community Report Card 2000* (North Dartmouth, MA: Center for Policy Analysis, 2000).

[50]Cf. Stephen L. Cabral, *Tradition and Transformation: Portuguese Feasting in New Bedford* (New York: AMS Press, 1989).

[51]Cf. Raymond Breton and Maurice Pinard, "Group Formation Among Immigrants: Criteria and Processes," *Canadian Journal of Economics and Political Science,*Vol. 26, No. 3 (August 1960): 465-77.

[52]The terms liberal and neo-liberal are employed in their contemporary "American" usage, rather than in their classical "European" meanings (see Dolbeare and Medcalf 1993, 72-83). Liberalism, in its American usage, is an ideological orientation that seeks to promote social justice and equity through state action while accepting the principle that such policies depend on the expansion and profitability of the private sector. This contrasts with American "conservatives," who advocate a laissez-faire economic policy or socialists who advocate public and social ownership of the means of production.

[53]Norman H. Nie, Sidney Verba, and John Petrocik, *The Changing American Voter* (Cambridge, MA: Harvard University Press, 1976); Everett Carl Ladd, *Where Have All the Voters Gone?: The Fracturing of America's Political Parties* (New York: W.W. Norton and Co., Inc., 1978).

[54]In Massachusetts (2000), there are 1,794,046 registered Democrats, 489,060 registered Republicans, and 1,909,451 registered Unenrolled voters (an Unenrolled voter in Massachusetts is called an Independent voter in most other states).

[55]The survey samples are not large enough to make definitive statements about the differences between u.s.-born and foreign-born Portuguese-Americans, but the apparent differences captured in the following chapters are striking. Indeed, on many items, the differences between foreign-born and u.s.-born Portuguese-Americans are larger than those between u.s.-born Portuguese-Americans and other Americans. There is no question that further research on this question will prove interesting, but the surveys reported in this book suggest tentatively at least that the Portuguese assimilate into American society rather quickly (i.e., by the second generation), particularly as educational and occupational attainment reach levels comparable to those of the average American.

CHAPTER 2

POLITICAL AND CIVIC PARTICIPATION OF PORTUGUESE-AMERICANS IN TAUNTON, MASSACHUSETTS

CLYDE W. BARROW, DAVID R. BORGES,
AND SHAWNA E. SWEENEY[1]

Methodology and Sample

Political and civic participation among Portuguese-Americans was surveyed in Census Tract 6137 of Taunton, Massachusetts, which was selected because it contains a high percentage of Portuguese-Americans and foreign-born residents of Portuguese origin. The City of Taunton has a total population of 49,832 (1990 U.S. Census). Census Tract 6137 is located in the central area of Taunton and has a total population of 4,482 (see Figure 1).[2] Nearly half (46.9%) of the census tract's residents are primarily of Portuguese ancestry and nearly one-fifth (19.3%) are foreign born. Almost a third (30.5%) of the census tract's residents primarily speak a language other than English (most frequently Portuguese).

FIGURE I

Census Tract 6137

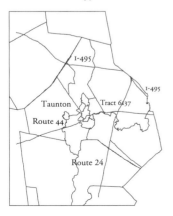

The census tract's residents are overwhelmingly white Caucasian (96.7%) with a sprinkling of African-American (1.1%) and Hispanic (1.9%) residents (See Table 1). This racial and ethnic mix is largely typical of Southeastern Massachusetts, although nearby cities such as Fall River and New Bedford have seen an influx of African-American, Asian, and Hispanic residents during the 1990s. The Portuguese constitute the single largest ancestry group in the census tract at 46.9 percent of the population, although it also contains significant groups of residents who identify their primary ancestry as Irish (16.3%), French (9.3%), English (6.9%), Polish (3.7%), Italian (2.5%), and German (2.3%) (see Table 2).

40

TABLE 1

CENSUS TRACT 6137: RACE AND ETHNICITY, 1990

Race Ethnicity	Number	Percent
White	4333	96.7%
Black	49	1.1%
Native American	0	0.0%
Asian	0	0.0%
Hispanic	87	1.9%
Other	13	0.3%
Total	4482	100.0%

SOURCE: U.S. CENSUS, 1990

TABLE 2

CENSUS TRACT 6137: ANCESTRY, 1990

Ancestry	Number	Percent
Portuguese	1957	46.9%
Irish	680	16.3%
French	387	9.3%
English	288	6.9%
Polish	154	3.7%
Italian	104	2.5%
German	98	2.3%
Other	506	12.1%
Total	4174	100.0%

SOURCE: U.S. CENSUS, 1990

The census tract's residents were surveyed in late 1999 and early 2000 using two survey instruments (see Appendix A), which were updated and modified versions of the survey instrument first used in the classic study, *Participation in America* (1972), by Sidney Verba and Norman H. Nie.[3] The first survey was administered by telephone, while the second was conducted through face-to-face interviews. Both surveys were administered exclusively to households in Census Tract 6137. The combined surveys obtained valid responses from one adult in 23.6 percent of the 1,710 households in Census Tract 6137.

The survey obtained a total of 404 valid responses from residents of Census Tract 6137 in Taunton, Massachusetts.[4] More than 40 percent (40.7%) of respondents identified themselves as Portuguese, compared to 46.9 percent who identified themselves as Portuguese in the 1990 U.S. Census. The average age of all respondents is 45.0 years, and respondents' median family income is between $35,000 and $45,000. Nearly four-fifths of respondents (78.0%) have at least a high school diploma, while 23.5 percent have a bachelor's degree or higher. The majority of respondents (55.0%) were female. In general, Portuguese-Americans had lower levels of educational attainment and lower incomes than non-Portuguese respondents (see Appendix A).

Citizenship, Voting, and Political Influence

Verba and Nie's (1972, 26-27) pioneering study confirmed "a rather standard and accepted picture" of political participation in the United States; namely, "low levels of citizen participation and the concentration of political activity in the hands of a small portion of the citizens."[5] Since Verba and Nie's study was conducted in 1972, participation in the most basic political activity – voting – has continued to decline in the United States, while citizen trust in government, corporations, labor unions, and other institutions has reached an all-time low.

Verba and Nie found that less than one-third of u.s. citizens had ever attempted to influence the voting decisions of others. Less than 10 percent of Americans had attended political meetings or rallies during an election. About 8 percent had donated money to political campaigns or causes, and no more than 5 percent belonged to a political club or local party organization. Similar studies have found that only about

41

one-quarter (28%) of U.S. citizens have ever attempted in any way to influence the outcome of a governmental decision in their local community, and fewer than 16 percent have made similar efforts at the national level. Furthermore, numerous studies consistently document that it is often the same people who participate across a range of different activities (see Table 3).

TABLE 3

Twelve Different Acts of Political Participation

Type of Political Participation	Percent
Report regularly voting in Presidential Elections	72%
Report always voting in local elections	47%
Active in at least one organization involved in community problems	32%
Have worked with others in trying to solve some community problems	30%
Have attempted to persuade others to vote as they were	28%
Have ever actively worked for a party or candidates during an election	26%
Have ever contacted a local government official about some issues or problems	20%
Have attended at least on political meeting or really in last 3 years	19%
Have ever contacted a local government offical about some issue or problem	18%
Have ever formed a group or organization to attempt to solve some local community problem	14%
Have ever given money to a party or candidate during an election campaign	13%
Presently a member of a political club or organization	8%

SOURCE: VERBA AND NIE (1972, 31)

However, broad studies of political participation and narrower studies of voting behavior consistently document that political participation is not evenly distributed among different groups and classes of U.S. citizens. Verba and Nie's work confirmed a standard socio-economic model of participation, which finds that the socio-economic status of an individual – occupation, education, and income – predicts to a large extent how much a person is likely to participate in politics. In other words, an attorney, business manager, or university professor is much more likely to engage in a broad range of political activities such as voting, lobbying, letter writing, and attendance at meetings than a sewing machine operator employed by an apparel factory. The higher a person's occupational status, the higher a person's educational attainment, and the higher a person's income, the more likely he or she is to be politically active and vice-versa.

While the socio-economic model continues to provide a baseline for expectations about political participation in America, there is a good deal of variance in the model because other social characteristics can intervene to cause "deviations" from the model's normal expectations. These other forces may lead specific individuals or groups of individuals to be more active than expected given their socio-economic characteristics. These factors can include generational effects (age), race or ethnicity, party affiliation, membership in voluntary associations, civic attitudes, and a sense of political efficacy. The survey respondents in Taunton, Massachusetts were asked several questions about citizenship, voting, and political influence to determine to what extent, if any, the political and civic behavior of Portuguese-Americans differs from that of other residents in Southeastern Massachusetts.

Are you a U.S. citizen?
Respondents were asked whether they are a United States citizen. Nearly all of the respondents (94.0%) are U.S. citizens (see Table 4). Only 6.0 percent of the respondents report that they are not U.S. citizens. This compares to a statewide average of 5.5 percent of Massachusetts residents who are not U.S. citizens. Of the 24 respondents who are not U.S. citizens, twenty-two were of Portuguese ancestry.

TABLE 4

Citizen?	Number	Percent
Yes	379	94.0%
No	24	6.0%

Are you registered to vote?
Respondents were asked if they are registered to vote. A large majority (87.8%) of respondents report they are registered to vote (see Table 5). This number is consistent with actual voter registration in Massachusetts, where approximately 86 percent of the voting age public (which includes non-citizens) was registered to vote at the time of the survey.[6] There is a small difference in voter registration levels between Portuguese and non-Portuguese respondents, with 85.9 percent of Portuguese respondents who are citizens reporting they are reg-

43

istered voters compared to 88.6 percent of non-Portuguese respondents. The percentage of all respondents who are registered to vote increases as their educational attainment level increases, which is consistent with the standard socio-economic model of voting behavior (see Figure 2). The correlation between educational attainment and voter registration among citizens is statistically significant and it holds true for both Portuguese and non-Portuguese citizens.

Portuguese-Americans who are not u.s. citizens are obviously not eligible to register to vote in the United States. However, since this group is 6.0 percent of the survey sample, and nearly 92 percent of non-citizens in the sample were of Portuguese ancestry, the findings understate significant differences in voter registration rates among the Portuguese. When non-citizens are included in the analysis, differences in rates of voter registration between Portuguese and non-Portuguese residents widen considerably, with 87.8 of the non-Portuguese group registered to vote compared to 74.1 percent of the Portuguese population (see Table 6). This difference constitutes a statistically significant correlation between ethnicity and the likelihood of voter registration.

TABLE 5

Registered to Vote?	All Respondents Number/Percent		Portuguese Percent	Non-Portuguese Percent
Yes	331	87.8%	85.9%	88.6%
No	46	12.2%	14.1%	11.4%

TABLE 6

Citizens and Non-Citizens Combined

Registered to Vote	All Respondents Number/Percent		Portuguese Percent	Non-Portuguese Percent
Yes	332	82.6	74.1	87.8
No	70	17.4	25.9	12.2

FIGURE 2

Are You Registared to Vote

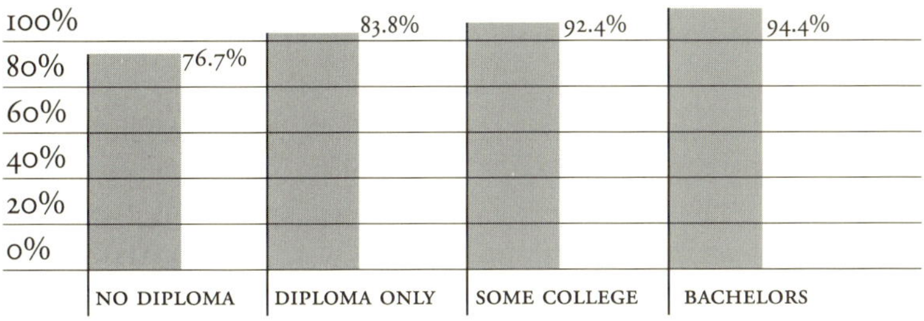

100%		83.8%	92.4%	94.4%
80%	76.7%			
60%				
40%				
20%				
0%				
	NO DIPLOMA	DIPLOMA ONLY	SOME COLLEGE	BACHELORS

The results suggest that as the Portuguese become u.s. citizens, they tend to register to vote in proportions similar to those of other residents in Massachusetts. For example, when only u.s. citizens are compared to each other, Portuguese-Americans constitute 41 percent of all non-registrants, which is roughly proportional to their numbers in the survey sample. However, when non-citizens are included in the group, the Portuguese constitute 58.6 percent of all non-registrants

Did you vote in the 1996 U.S. Presidential election?

Respondents were asked if they voted in the 1996 U.S. Presidential election. Three-quarters of the respondents (75.0%) who are citizens say they voted in the 1996 U.S. Presidential election, while 25.0 percent did not vote (see Table 7). Slightly fewer Portuguese (72.6%) than non-Portuguese (76.4%) report voting in the 1996 election. When non-citizens are included in the sample, the difference obviously widens by a considerable margin. A total of 70.2% of the voting age population, which includes non-citizens, report voting in the 1996 Presidential election. When all persons of voting age (including non-citizens) are included in the analysis, then 62.0 percent of voting-age Portuguese voted in the u.s. Presidential election compared to 75.8 percent of the non-Portuguese population.

TABLE 7

Vote in 1996?	All Respondents Number Percent		Portuguese Percent	Non-Portuguese Percent
Yes	274	75.0%	72.6%	76.4%
No	75	25.0%	27.4%	23.6%

Respondents (citizens only) with a bachelor's degree or higher were most likely to vote in the 1996 U.S. Presidential election (89.5%), while respondents with a high school diploma or less report voting in the 1996 U.S. Presidential election with less frequency (65.1%). These results are not only consistent with the socio-economic model of voting behavior, the findings suggest that lower levels of voter registration and voting among the Portuguese are strongly correlated with their lower levels of educational attainment. These correlations and the differences they measure are obviously much larger when non-citizens are included in the sample. In addition, a higher percentage of respondents who get their information about politics and government from newspapers voted in the 1996 presidential election than those who rely on other sources of information, such as radio and television, and this result is also statistically significant.

How often do you vote in local elections?
Respondents who are citizens were asked how often they vote in local elections. Fewer than half (43.7%) report that they always vote in local elections, while another 29.3 percent report that they sometimes miss a local election (see Table 8). More than a quarter (27.0%) of respondents report that they rarely or never vote in local elections. When non-citizens are included in the analysis, then 31.3 percent of respondents report that they rarely or never vote in local elections.

An interesting finding is that a higher percentage of Portuguese respondents (54.5%) report that they always vote in local elections in comparison to non-Portuguese respondents (37.9%), and this result is statistically significant. It is also consistent with responses to other questions which reveal that Portuguese-Americans are more interested in local politics than in national politics and with the fact that Taunton had a Portuguese-American mayor and a Portuguese-American state senator at the time of the survey. There is a statistically significant relationship between respondents' membership in political groups and civic organizations and how often respondents vote in local elections. Respondents who get their political information from newspapers are also more likely to vote in local elections than other respondents.

TABLE 8

How Often Do You Vote in Local Elections?	All Respondents Number/Percent		Portuguese Percent	Non-Portuguese Percent
always vote	164	43.7%	54.5%	37.9%
sometimes miss one	110	29.3%	19.4%	34.5%
rarely vote	34	9.1%	6.7%	10.6%
never vote	67	17.9%	19.4%	17.0%

During elections, how often do you try to persuade people as to why they should vote for one of the parties or candidates?

47

Respondents were asked whether they try to influence how other people vote in elections by persuading them to vote for a particular party or candidate. The majority of respondents (53.2%) report that they never try to influence others' voting behavior. Only 11.7 percent of the respondents often try to influence how others vote (see Table 9). A majority of Portuguese (53.0%) and non-Portuguese (53.4%) respondents never try to influence how other people vote. A slightly higher percentage of Portuguese respondents (35.6%) will often or sometimes try to persuade other people how to vote compared to non-Portuguese respondents (29.4%).

TABLE 9

Try to Persuade People?	All Respondents Number/Percent		Portuguese Percent	Non-Portuguese Percent
Often	46	11.7%	14.4%	9.7%
sometimes	80	20.4%	22.7%	19.4%
rarely	58	14.8%	12.1%	17.3%
never	209	53.2%	50.8%	53.6%

There are several statistically significant relationships regarding how often respondents try to persuade people during elections. Respondents with higher incomes are more likely to try to persuade people than are respondents with lower incomes. Respondents who belong to political organizations are more likely to try to persuade people during elections than those who do not belong to political organizations. Respondents who get their information from newspapers are more likely to try to persuade people how to vote than those who get their information from other sources.

How much influence do you think people have over local government?
Respondents were asked how much influence they think people have over local government. Nearly half (46.8%) of all respondents feel that people have a lot (17.0%) or a moderate amount (29.8%) of influence over local government, while only 17.0 percent feel that people have no influence over local government (see Table 10). A higher percentage of Portuguese respondents (20.6%) indicate that people can have a lot of influence over local government in comparison to non-Portuguese respondents (13.8%), but paradoxically Portuguese respondents are also more likely to feel that people have no influence over local government. There is a statistically significant correlation between Portuguese ethnicity and feelings that one can influence local government, although it is not possible based on the geographically confined sample to determine whether these results are peculiar to Taunton or more widely applicable to Southeastern Massachusetts. There is also a statistically significant correlation between education and the view that one can influence government (see Figure 3). Respondents who belong to political organizations and those who get their political information from newspapers are also more likely than other respondents to feel that people have a lot or a moderate amount of influence over local government.

TABLE 10

Influence Over Local Government	All Respondents Number/Percent		Portuguese Percent	Non-Portuguese Percent
a lot	68	17.0%	20.6%	13.8%
a moderate amount	119	29.8%	21.9%	35.1%
some amount	142	35.5%	35.5%	36.4%
none at all	68	17.0%	20.6%	14.2%
don't know	3	0.8%	1.3%	0.4%

FIGURE 3

How Much Influence Do People Have
Over Local Government

Respondents Indicating "A Lot" or "A Moderate Amount"

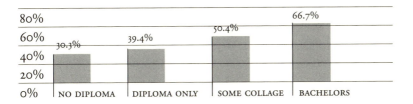

How interested are you in politics and national affairs?

Respondents were asked about their level of interest in politics and national affairs. Nearly two-thirds of respondents (64.4%) report that they are very or somewhat interested in politics and national affairs (see Table 11). Only 13.7 percent of respondents are not interested in politics and national affairs. Non-Portuguese respondents are much more likely to be very or somewhat interested in politics and national affairs (71.0%) compared to Portuguese respondents (54.4%), and this difference is statistically significant.

Respondents with higher levels of educational attainment are also more likely to be interested in politics and national affairs than are respondents with lower levels of education. Respondents with higher incomes and respondents who belong to various groups or organizations such as fraternal and nationality groups are also more likely to be interested in politics and national affairs than are other respondents. Interest in politics and national affairs also increases among persons who belong to more than one civic group. These findings are consistent with the standard socio-economic model, but they also suggest that non-partisan and non-political civic organizations may have the capacity to increase overall levels of political participation without necessarily influencing the partisan or ideological character of participation.

Where do you get your information about politics and government?

Respondents were asked where they get their information about politics and government. Seven choices were provided to the respondents, who were allowed to give more than one response. Respondents are most likely to get their information about politics and government from television (80.2%) and newspapers (68.8%), although large percentages receive information from radio (40.8%) and friends (34.9%). Few respondents receive political information from employers, unions, or churches (see Table 12).

TABLE 11

Interest in Politics & National Affairs	All Respondents Number/Percent		Portuguese Percent	Non-Portuguese Percent
very interested	85	21.1%	13.9%	25.6%
somewhat interested	174	43.3%	40.5%	45.4%
only slightly interested	88	21.9%	25.9%	19.7%
not at all interested	55	13.7%	19.6%	9.2%

TABLE 12

Where Do You Get Info About Politics?	All Respondents Number/Percent		Portuguese Percent	Non-Portuguese Percent
television	324	80.2%	84.2%	77.9%
newspapers	278	68.8%	58.9%	75.0%
radio	165	40.8%	41.8%	40.4%
friends	141	34.9%	36.7%	33.8%
unions	31	7.7%	4.4%	9.2%
church	21	5.2%	5.1%	4.6%
employer	32	7.9%	10.1%	5.8%

Portuguese respondents are slightly more inclined to receive information about government and politics from television than are non-Portuguese respondents. Non-Portuguese respondents are more likely to receive political information from newspapers than the Portuguese and this is a statistically significant correlation. The result may again be explained by the lower levels of literacy and educational attainment among Portuguese-Americans.

Educated respondents are more likely to get their information about politics and government from newspapers than are less educated respondents. Respondents with higher incomes are also more likely to get their information about politics and government from newspapers than are respondents with lower incomes, while respondents with lower incomes are more likely to get their information from television. Respondents who belong to political organizations or civic groups are also more likely to get their information from newspapers, friends, and unions than are respondents who do not belong to a political organization or civic group, which suggests that civic organizations contribute to the flow of political information among members and that low levels of civic involvement will be associated with low levels of political information.

Measures of Civic Activity

To what types of organizations do you belong?

Respondents were asked whether they belong to several different types of voluntary organizations and civic associations. Respondents are most likely to belong to church groups, sports groups, and professional or academic societies (see Table 13). "Other" responses volunteered by those interviewed include the Boy Scouts, National Rifle Association, musical groups, and senior citizen groups. In general, similar percentages of Portuguese and non-Portuguese respondents belong to each group, although non-Portuguese respondents are more likely to be members of an academic or professional society. The latter is the only

TABLE 13

Belong to Which Organizations	All Respondents Number/Percent		Portuguese Percent	Non-Portuguese Percent
church affiliated groups	99	24.5%	23.4%	25.8%
sports groups	73	18.1%	17.7%	17.5%
professional/academic societies	58	14.4%	9.5%	17.1%
labor unions	49	12.1%	10.8%	12.5%
youth groups	40	9.9%	9.5%	10.0%
nationality groups	35	8.7%	10.8%	7.1%
fraternal groups	28	6.9%	7.0%	6.7%
veterans' groups	21	5.2%	3.2%	5.8%
service clubs	20	5.0%	6.3%	4.2%
other	20	5.0%	4.4%	5.4%
political clubs	15	3.7%	5.1%	2.9%

significant difference in group membership and it is probably explained by differences in educational attainment and occupational status.

Community Involvement

Respondents were asked to rate their level of community involvement on a scale from 1 to 5. A person who was least involved in their community was ranked as a 1, while a person who was most involved was ranked as a 5. Respondents report that overall they are not very involved in their community (see Table 14). Only 17.9 percent of respondents ranked their level of community service as a 4 or 5 (i.e., high), and there is no significant difference between the answers of Portuguese and non-Portuguese respondents. However, respondents who belong to political groups view themselves as more active in the community, as do respondents who get their political information from newspapers.

TABLE 14

COMMUNITY INVOLVEMENT

Scale	All Respondents Number/Percent		Portuguese Percent	Non-Portuguese Percent
1	94	23.7%	20.0%	26.7%
2	87	22.0%	17.4%	24.6%
3	144	36.4%	40.0%	33.5%
4	39	9.8%	12.3%	8.5%
5	32	8.1%	10.3%	6.8%

Political Information

Respondents were asked to name various political leaders and officeholders in their community. In general, respondents have low levels of political knowledge based on this simple measurement. For example, more than a third of the respondents (38.6%) do not know the name of the mayor of Taunton and almost a third of the respondents (32.4%) do not know the name of the Governor of Massachusetts. There were only small differences between the responses of Portuguese and non-Portuguese respondents, although Portuguese respondents are less likely to be able to name the Governor of Massachusetts than are non-Portuguese respondents.

What is the name of the Mayor of Taunton?

Respondents were asked if they could name the Mayor of Taunton. More than a third of the respondents (38.6%) do not know the name of the Mayor of Taunton (see Table 15). Although the Mayor of Taunton changed while the face-to-face interviews were being conducted, the data takes this fact into account. There is no significant difference between the responses of Portuguese and non-Portuguese respondents. Respondents with higher levels of education and those who get their political information from newspapers are more likely to know the name of the Mayor of Taunton.

53

TABLE 15

Know Name of Taunton Mayor	All Respondents Number/Percent		Portuguese Percent	Non-Portuguese Percent
correct response	248	61.4%	60.1%	61.7%
incorrect response	53	13.1%	15.2%	12.1%
don't know	103	25.5%	24.7%	26.3%

What is the name of the Governor of Massachusetts?

Respondents were asked if they could name the Governor of Massachusetts. Almost a third of the respondents (32.4%) do not know the name of the Governor of Massachusetts (see Table 16). The results are particularly notable, since during the time the survey was being conducted, the Governor's name was displayed prominently in all forms of the news media as the result of a scandal about $1.4 billion in cost overruns on the Central Artery highway project. Portuguese respondents are less likely to know the name of the governor of Massachusetts than are non-Portuguese respondents and this is a statistically significant difference. Respondents with higher levels of education are more likely to be able to name the Governor of Massachusetts. Respondents with higher incomes, respondents who belong to political groups, and respondents who get their political information from newspapers are also more likely to know the name of the Governor than are respondents with the opposite characteristics and these results are statistically significant.

TABLE 16

Know Name of Governor	All Respondents Number/Percent		Portuguese Percent	Non-Portuguese Percent
correct response	273	67.6%	53.8%	76.3%
incorrect response	17	4.2%	5.7%	3.3%
don't know	114	28.2%	40.5%	20.4%

What are the names of the U.S. Senators from Massachusetts?

Fewer than half (42.7%) of the respondents are able to identify both United States Senators from Massachusetts (see Table 17). There is no statistically significant difference, based on ethnicity, between the percentage of respondents who know or do not know the names of the U.S. Senators from Massachusetts. However, respondents with higher incomes, respondents who belong to political groups, and respondents who get their political information from newspapers are more likely to know the name of the U.S. Senators from Massachusetts than are other respondents and these results are statistically significant.

TABLE 17

Know Name of U.S. Senators	All Respondents Number/Percent		Portuguese Percent	Non-Portuguese Percent
correct response	172	42.7%	42.0%	43.3%
one correct response	128	31.8%	25.5%	35.4%
incorrect response	19	4.8%	5.7%	4.2%
don't know	84	20.8%	26.8%	17.1%

What is the name of the U.S. Congressman from your district?

Only slightly less than a third of the respondents (32.4%) are able to name the U.S. Congressman from their district (see Table 18). There is no significant difference between Portuguese and non-Portuguese respondents in being able to identify the U.S. Congressman from their district. However, the more educated the respondents, the more likely they are to be able to identify their u.s. Congressman and vice-versa. Respondents who belong to political groups and respondents who get their political information from newspapers are also more likely to know the name of the u.s. Congressman from their district.

TABLE 18

Know Name of U.S. Congressman	All Respondents Number/Percent		Portuguese Percent	Non-Portuguese Percent
correct response	131	32.4%	30.4%	33.3%
incorrect response	41	10.1%	12.7%	8.3%
don't know	232	57.4%	57.0%	58.3%

What is the name of the State Senator who represents Taunton?

More than half of the respondents (54.5%) do not know the name of the State Senator who represents Taunton (see Table 19). There is no significant difference between the ability of Portuguese and non-Portuguese respondents to name their State Senator. More highly educated respondents, those who belong to political groups, and those who get their political information from newspapers are more likely to know the name of their state senator than other respondents.

TABLE 19

Know Name of State Senator	All Respondents Number/Percent		Portuguese Percent	Non-Portuguese Percent
correct response	183	45.5%	47.5%	43.7%
incorrect response	25	6.2%	7.6%	5.5%
don't know	194	48.3%	44.9%	50.8%

What is the name of the State Representative for your area?

Over seventy percent of respondents (71.3%) do not know the name of their state representative (see Table 20). There is no significant difference between the ability of Portuguese and non-Portuguese respondents to name their state representative. However, respondents with higher levels of education are better able to identify the state representative from their district. Respondents with higher incomes, respondents who belong to political groups, and respondents who get their political information from newspapers are also more likely to know the name of their state representative than are other respondents and these correlations are significant.

TABLE 20

Know Name of State Representative	All Respondents Number/Percent		Portuguese Percent	Non-Portuguese Percent
correct response	113	28.7%	27.8%	28.3%
incorrect response	30	7.4%	10.8%	5.0%
don't know	258	63.9%	61.4%	66.7%

Key Informant Interviews

A long form survey was administered exclusively to Portuguese respondents in Census Tract 6137, while a short form survey was given to non-Portuguese respondents. Both surveys contained an identical set of questions (short form) pertaining to political and civic participation, although the long form included additional questions that probe the reasons for participation and non-participation among Portuguese-Americans. The long form included a significant number of open-ended questions designed to elicit spontaneous answers from respondents. The results presented below include data that appeared only on the long form survey (Portuguese respondents). A total of 104 face-to-face interviews were completed and fifty-five (52.9%) of these persons were of Portuguese ancestry.

Demographic Profile

In the key informant interviews, nearly fifty-three percent (52.9%) of respondents were of Portuguese ancestry. More than half of the respondents are male (52.7%), while 47.3 percent of the respondents are female. All but two of the 55 respondents are Catholic (96.4%). The average age of respondents is 47.0 years and their median family income is between $35,000 and $45,000. However, nearly half of the respondents (46.7%) have an annual family income below $35,000 (see Table 21). More than a third of respondents (35.3%) are employed in blue collar jobs such as machine operator and assembly occupations (see Table 22), while 13.7 percent report being unemployed at a time when the Massachusetts and local economies were at full employment.

TABLE 21

Annual Family Income	Number	Percent
less than $15,000	4	8.5%
$15,000 to $25,000	9	19.1%
$25,000 to $35,000	9	19.1%
$35,000 to $45,000	8	17.0%
$45,000 to $60,000	10	21.3%
$60,000 to $150,000	7	14.9%
$150,000 or more	0	0.0%

TABLE 22

Occupation	Number	Percent
White Collar		
executive/managerial	3	5.9%
professional	1	2.0%
technicians and related occupations	4	7.8%
Total:	8	15.79%
Blue Collar		
precision production, crafts, repair	5	9.8%
machine operator/inspector/assembler	10	19.6%
transportation/moving	2	3.9%
handlers/helpers	1	2.0%
Total:	18	35.39%
Service		
service occupations	10	19.6%
private household	4	7.8%
Total:	14	27.49%
Other		
unemployed	7	13.7%
retired	4	7.8%
Total:	11	21.59%

Fewer than half of the respondents (41.8%) have a high school diploma and a third (33.3%) have completed only four years of formal schooling, which was the minimum requirement in Portugal until 1968. Respondents were also asked where they completed their last grade of school. Nearly half (48.9%) of respondents finished their last year of school in Portugal. The remainder of the respondents report completing their last grade of school in the United States. Nearly all of the respondents (94.5%) indicate that they speak English, although only 55.5 percent of these respondents claim that they speak English well or very well (see Table 23). Respondents with higher levels of education are able to speak English better than less educated respondents (see Figure 4).

TABLE 23

Ability to Speak English	Number	Percent
very well	24	44.4%
well	6	11.1%
satisfactorily	13	24.1%
poorly	11	20.4%

TABLE 24

LENGTH OF RESIDENCY IN THE U.S.

Years in U.S.	Number	Percent
0 to 10	2	3.6%
11 to 20	5	9.1%
21 to 30	24	43.6%
31 to 40	19	34.5%
41 to 50	5	9.1%

FIGURE 4

ABILITY TO SPEAK ENGLISH VERY WELL BY EDUCATION LEVEL

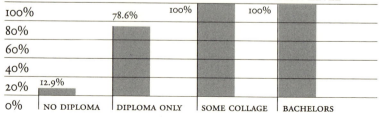

The vast majority (96.4%) of long-form respondents in Census Tract 6137 have been in the United States for more than 21 years (see Table 24). Only two respondents have been in the country for fewer than ten years. Thus, nearly all of the survey respondents have had time to learn English and to become familiar with the American political system and political culture on the local, state, and national levels. The respondents have also had time to become familiar with Taunton and its political groups, since 82 percent have lived in the City of Taunton for at least 21 years.

Citizenship

Are you a citizen?
Thirteen (23.6%) of the fifty-five key informants were not United States citizens. These thirteen respondents are all citizens of Portugal. Only one of the non-citizen respondents has applied for United States citizenship. When asked why they have not become citizens of the United States, the majority of respondents cited "other" reasons (see Table 25). These other reasons include responses such as they "don't know how to read or write," "have no time" to apply for citizenship, and simply "never thought about it." Only 7.7 percent (N=1) of non-citizens have ever bothered to apply for citizenship.

TABLE 25

Why are You Not a Citizen?	*Number*	*Percent*
do not speak English	3	25.0%
do not know how to apply	0	0.0%
plan to return to home country	0	0.0%
do not want to	1	8.3%
other	8	66.7%

Are you interested in becoming a citizen?
The Portuguese who are not citizens of the United States were asked if they are interested in becoming United States citizens. All but one of the respondents answered in the affirmative (see Table 26).

TABLE 26

Are You Interested in Citizenship?	Number	Percent
Yes	12	92.3%
No	1	7.7%

Voting and Political Participation

Verba and Nie identified several different types of political and civic participation in the United States, including the voting specialist (21%), campaigners (15%), and parochial participants (4%). Verba and Nie define voting specialists as individuals who always vote in U.S. Presidential elections and in most local or state elections, but who do not engage in any other type of political activity. Campaigners are engaged heavily in political campaigns and campaign work, but they are not likely to engage in non-political forms of civic or communal activity. Finally, parochial participants are individuals who tend to vote only on issues that directly affect them (e.g., tax referenda) and who do not participate in political campaigns, but they do make particularized contacts with government officials on issues that directly affect them (e.g., garbage collection, property taxes). The survey results in Taunton suggest that Portuguese-Americans tend to be voting specialists, although in comparison to national figures a much larger percentage of Portuguese-Americans are also parochial participants.

Are you registered to vote?

Nearly eighty-four percent (83.7%) of the long-form respondents indicate that they are registered to vote (see Table 27), which is consistent with statewide voter registration levels in Massachusetts. When respondents who are not citizens of the United States are included in the data, then the number of Portuguese-Americans who are registered to vote falls to 63.6 percent, which is far below the statewide voter registration level.

TABLE 27

Registered to Vote?	Number	Percent
Yes	36	83.7%
No	7	16.3%

Why are you not registered to vote?

Respondents who are not registered to vote were asked why they are not registered (see Table 28). Persons who are not citizens of the United States are not eligible to register to vote. However, among the Portuguese-Americans who are U.S. citizens, a variety of reasons were offered, including they do not know how to register, they do not have time to register, they cannot read or write well, or they simply have not done it.

TABLE 28

Why Are You Not Registered?	Number	Percent
do not know how to register	1	14.3
not interested in politics	1	14.3
no time to register	1	14.3
cannot read well	1	14.3
have not got around to it	2	28.6
application denied	1	14.3

Are you interested in registering to vote?

Other than those persons who are not interested in politics, the vast majority (85.7%) of Portuguese-Americans who are not registered to vote indicate that they are interested in registering (see Table 29).

TABLE 29

Interested in Registering?	Number	Percent
Yes	6	85.7%
No	1	14.3%

In what party are you registered?

Respondents were asked if they are registered with a political party and, if so, which political party (see Table 30). Nearly two-thirds of respondents identify themselves as Democrats (64.7%). None identified themselves as Republicans and 11.4 percent were "unenrolled."[7] A significant number of respondents refused to answer the question (N=20).

TABLE 30

Registered Party	Number	Percent
Democrat	22	64.7%
Republican	0	0.0%
Unenrolled	4	11.8%
Refused to declare	8	23.5%
Other	0	0.0%

Respondents were also asked why they identify with their party. The majority of the open-ended responses are that Portuguese-Americans identify with the Democratic party's traditional liberal ideology. The open-ended responses include:

- Better party/liked party's ideology
- (Party) better for workers or poor
- Spouse/parents members of party
- Democratic principles
- Friends registered in party
- Kennedy reputation good for immigrants

Do you have strong party ties?

Respondents who are Democrats (none identified themselves as Republican) were also asked to indicate how strongly they identify with the party. Nearly three-quarters (71.4%) of the respondents who are Democrats identify strongly with the party (see Table 31). Respondents who are "unenrolled" were asked to indicate whether they are closer to the Democratic or the Republican Party. All of these respondents (100%) identify themselves as closer to the Democratic Party (N=4).

TABLE 31

Party Ties	Number	Percent
strong ties	15	71.4%
not very strong ties	6	28.6%

Did you vote in the 1996 U.S. Presidential election?

Respondents were asked who they voted for in the 1996 U.S.

Presidential election. Over eighty-percent (80.6%) of those who responded to the question report that they voted in the 1996 Presidential election (N=29), although a large number of individuals refused to answer the question. When non-respondents are included in the sample, voter turn-out drops to 69 percent of Portuguese-Americans who are u.s. citizens and 52.7 percent of the Portuguese-American voting age population (including non-citizens).[8]

Nearly all (96.6%) of the Portuguese-American respondents who voted in the 1996 u.s. Presidential election report that they voted for Bill Clinton, which is consistent with the survey's findings that Portuguese-Americans have exceptionally strong loyalties to the Democratic Party. Respondents were also asked why they voted for a particular candidate. Most responses relate to the personal characteristics of candidates and their style of communication, while ideology, the economy, and public policy play an important but secondary role. Open-ended responses on why Portuguese-Americans voted for Bill Clinton include:

63

- Thought he was the best candidate/Liked him better
- Because he's a Democrat
- Doing a good job in office
- The way he talked, communicated with people
- Liked his policy
- Doesn't know/doesn't remember
- Thought Clinton would be better for him
- Because of the economy
- Consistent with my ideology
- Believe in his possibilities as a candidate

Who did you vote for in the 1992 U.S. Presidential election?

Respondents were asked whether they voted in the 1992 u.s. Presidential election. Over eighty-five percent (85.7%) of those who responded to the question report that they voted in the 1992 presidential election (N=28), although a large number of individuals refused to answer the question. When non-respondents are included in the sample, voter turn-out drops to 57 percent of Portuguese-Americans who are u.s. citizens and 43.6 percent of the Portuguese-American voting age population (including non-citizens).[9]

Respondents were then asked who they voted for in the 1992 U.S. Presidential election. Nearly all respondents who voted in 1992 cast their ballot for Bill Clinton (75.0%), while 7.1 percent voted for George Bush, 10.7% did not vote, and one respondent voted for another candidate. Respondents were also asked why they voted for a particular candidate. The reasons why individuals report voting for Bill Clinton in 1992 include:

- Because he's a Democrat
- His program/platform
- Better candidate
- Need a change
- Disliked Bush
- More qualified than Bush
- Need a national health service
- The way he talked, communicated with people

Have you contributed money to a political party or candidate?

Voter turnout among Portuguese-Americans who are registered to vote is comparable to that of other groups in the United States and Massachusetts, but respondents tend to specialize in voting and do not generally participate in other aspects of a political campaign. For example, fewer than ten percent (9.1%) of respondents have contributed money to a political party, a candidate, or to a political cause in the past four years (see Table 32). Even though non-citizens are prohibited from voting, they are not prohibited from making a campaign contribution, nor are they prohibited from volunteering to work in a political campaign.

TABLE 32

Contributed Money?	Number	Percent
Yes	5	9.1%
No	50	90.9%

Have you ever done work for a party or candidate?
Fewer than a fifth (19.5%) of Portuguese-American respondents have ever worked for a political party or candidate (see Table 33). Only 1.8 percent report belonging to an organized political group such as a Democratic or Republican Club or a political action committee. However, about one-fifth (21.3%) of the 55 Portuguese-American respondents indicate they are interested in becoming more involved in politics such as helping with a candidate's campaign (N=2) or voting (N=5).

TABLE 33

Done Work for Party Or Candidate?	Number	Percent
most elections	0	0.0%
some elections	5	9.3%
only a few elections	5	9.3%
never done such work	44	81.5%

Contact with government officials
The long-form survey asked whether respondents have ever contacted government officials with a particular concern. More than a fifth (22.2%) of the respondents report contacting a government official in Taunton about some need or problem in the past year, while 29.5 percent of u.s. citizens have initiated parochial contacts. This is much higher than Nie and Verba's findings (4%) for the nation as a whole. The range of particularized contacts include the mayor, city councilor, state representative, and state senator.

These findings are also consistent with Portuguese-American's greater interest in local politics, since only half this number (11.1%) have ever contacted a government official outside of Taunton, including the u.s. Congressional Representative or u.s. Senator. In both cases, 100 percent of the non-citizens responding to this question indicate that they have never contacted a government official at any level of government.

How often do you attend City Council meetings?
Respondents were asked how often they attend City Council meetings in the City of Taunton. More than half of the respondents (58.2%)

never attend City Council meetings and no respondents attend meetings regularly (see Table 34). Only 7.3 percent report that they sometimes attend a City Council meeting, while 34.5 percent rarely attend a City Council meeting.

TABLE 34

How Often Attend Council Meetings?	Number	Percent
always attend	0	0.0%
sometimes attend	4	7.3%
rarely attend	19	34.5%
never attend	32	58.2%

Political discussion

The long form survey also asked two questions about respondents' political activities in non-formal environments, such as talking with friends, watching television, and listening to radio talk shows. In general, the Portuguese-Americans surveyed in Taunton do not discuss politics and national affairs on a regular basis. Almost three-quarters (73.1%) of respondents discuss politics and national affairs less than once a week or never (see Table 35), while almost seventy percent (69.1%) report discussing local community problems with others less than once a week or never (see Table 36). As with other items, the higher the respondents' education, the more likely they are to discuss politics and national affairs.

Communal Activity

In their seminal study on *Participation in America,* Verba and Nie found that many Americans (20%) are "communalists," rather than political activists. Communalists are individuals who actively participate in civic affairs, but who avoid conflict and controversy (i.e., politics). Instead, they support and interact with the community by participating in consensus-based civic organizations, charities, and other forms of non-political action. The long-form survey asked two questions about respondents' participation in civic and community affairs.

In general, the majority of Portuguese-American respondents are not community or civic activists. For example, fewer than a fifth

(18.5%) of respondents report having worked to solve a community problem. Fewer than a tenth (9.3%) of the respondents have ever taken part in forming a new group or a new organization to try to solve a community problem. Very few (3.8%) of the respondents have ever personally gone to see, spoken to, or written to any community group about some need or problem in their community (including City Hall or a school organization).

TABLE 35

How Often Discuss Politics and National Affairs?	Number	Percent
every day	2	3.8%
once/twice a week	12	23.1%
less than once a week	20	38.5%
never	18	34.6%

TABLE 36

How Often Discuss Community Problems?	Number	Percent
every day	5	9.1%
once/twice a week	12	21.8%
less than once a week	20	36.4%
never	18	32.7%

Sources of Political and Civic Information

Respondents were asked a series of questions about the types of news magazines and newspapers they read and the television news shows they watch to obtain political and civic information. Fewer than a tenth (9.3%) of the respondents read news magazines regularly (e.g. *Newsweek, Time, U.S. News and World Report*). The magazines these respondents read most frequently are *Newsweek* and *Time*. However, nearly two-thirds (63.6%) of respondents read Portuguese language magazines or newspapers, watch Portuguese language television, or listen to Portuguese language radio (see Table 37). The media outlets most frequently identified by Taunton respondents are the *Portuguese Times, O Jornal*, RTPI-TV, and WJFD-FM radio.

TABLE 37

Read Portuguese Newspapers or Watch Portuguese New Shows?	Number	Percent
Yes	35	63.6%
No	20	36.4%

Respondents were also asked how often they watch television news broadcasts. Nearly three-quarters (72.2%) of the respondents watch television news every day, while another 24.1 percent watch television news at least a few times a week (see Table 38). The major sources for television news reported among respondents are NBC, CBS, PBS, CNN, CNBC, RTPI, and various local news channels based in Boston and Providence.

TABLE 38

How Often Do You Watch News?	Number	Percent
every day	39	72.2%
few times a week	13	24.1%
once a week	2	3.7%
never	0	0.0%

Respondents were also asked how often they read the newspaper. Sixty percent (60.0%) of respondents read the newspaper at least a few times a week (see Table 39). The newspapers most frequently read by respondents are the *Taunton Daily Gazette, Portuguese Times, Boston Herald, Boston Globe, Brockton Enterprise,* and *Providence Journal-Bulletin.*

TABLE 39

How Often Do You Read the Newspaper?	Number	Percent
every day	23	41.8%
few times a week	10	18.2%
once a week	11	20.0%
never	11	20.0%

Respondents are less likely to listen to talk radio than they are to watch television news or to read the newspaper (see Table 40). Just over one-quarter of respondents (27.8%) listen to talk radio at least a few times a week, while 38.9% never listen to talk radio. The stations that respondents listen to most frequently are wjfd (New Bedford), wbz (Boston), npr (Boston), weei (Boston), and wpep (Taunton). Only 4.4 percent of respondents have ever called a talk radio show.

TABLE 40

How Often Do You Listen to Talk Radio?	Number	Percent
every day	9	15.8
few times a week	7	12.3
once a week	7	12.3
less than once a week	22	38.6
never	12	21.1

TABLE 41

Perceived Influence Over Government	Local	State	Federal
a lot	18.9%	9.8%	12.0%
a moderate amount	7.5%	9.8%	8.0%
some amount	47.2%	51.0%	36.0%
none at all	26.4%	29.4%	44.0%

Political Efficacy

The long form survey asked several questions about respondents' sense of political efficacy. Political efficacy is the "belief that one can influence the political process. It is a feeling that an active citizen can play a part in bringing about social and political change, and that one's input counts."[10] Verba and Nie found that the higher the sense of political efficacy, the greater the likelihood that a person will participate in more demanding political activities. Conversely, a low sense of political efficacy is usually correlated with political apathy.

How much influence do people have over local, state, and federal government?

Respondents were asked how much influence they can have over the local, state, and federal governments. The Portuguese-Americans interviewed feel that they can most influence government at the local level, with only 26.4 percent feeling that they have no influence over local government. A slightly larger proportion (29.4%) feel that they have no influence over state government, while 44 percent feel that they have no influence over the federal government (see Table 41).

Attention from government officials

Respondents were asked how much attention an official from the local, state, or federal governments would give them if they had a complaint (see Table 42). In general, the amount of attention respondents expect to receive declines from the local to the federal government. Nearly a third (30.6%) expect to receive a lot of attention from local officials, while only 14.0 percent expect to receive a lot of attention from federal officials.

TABLE 42

How Much Attention from Government Officials?	Local	State	Federal
a lot of attention	30.6%	22.4%	14.0%
some attention	46.9%	40.8%	32.0%
very little attention	16.3%	24.5%	34.0%
no attention	4.1%	10.2%	16.0%

Respondents were also asked if they would need to find an intermediary or political connection to help them contact a government official. Nearly three-quarters of respondents (71.2%) indicate that they would need an intermediary or political connection (see Table 43), while 23.1 percent feel comfortable contacting a government official directly.

TABLE 43

Need a Connection?	Number	Percent
need a connection	37	71.2%
could contact directly	12	23.1%
don't know	3	5.8%

Ideology

Respondents were asked several questions about various issues to assess their political ideology. A "political ideology" is a pattern of beliefs, where a person's viewpoints on different issues are connected to each other by a set of basic principles.[11] In the United States, most persons are classified as either liberal or conservative, with liberals more likely to favor an active role for government in the economy and an active role in assisting the poor and the disadvantaged. In other words, liberals are more likely to believe that government is responsible for insuring equal opportunity to citizens, providing assistance to those who are least advantaged, and insuring an equitable distribution of income, while conservatives are more likely to favor "free market" and individual solutions to most problems. Respondents to the long-form survey were asked several questions designed to measure their liberal or conservative propensities. In general, the Portuguese-Americans surveyed in Taunton gravitate strongly toward liberalism and this finding is confirmed in the economic issues survey included as Chapter 4.

Aged, Unemployed, and Housing

Respondents were first asked who they thought was responsible for the aged, unemployment problems, and for adequate housing (Table 44). More than half of respondents (56.6%) feel that it is a family's responsibility to look after the aged, while a large majority feel it is government's role to solve unemployment problems (77.4%) and to guarantee adequate housing (63.3%) – although there were considerable differences concerning what level of government was responsible for these policies.

TABLE 44

Party Responsible	Looking Out for the Aged	Unemployment Problems	Providing Adequate Housing
individual and family	56.6%	13.2%	32.7%
local government	7.5%	18.9%	18.4%
state government	11.3%	32.1%	38.8%
federal government	20.8%	26.4%	6.1%
private groups	3.8%	1.9%	2.0%

Income Disparity

Respondents were asked about differences of income between the rich and poor and whether they think such differences are too great or as it should be. Nine-tenths (90.9%) of the respondents consider the gap between rich and poor too great, while more than half (50.9%) consider it "much too great" (see Table 45). Less than a tenth of respondents (9.1%) feel that the income gap is as it should be.

TABLE 45

Income Gap	Number	Percent
much too great	28	50.9%
great	12	21.8%
somewhat too great	10	18.2%
as it should be	5	9.1%

Needs of Poor

Respondents were asked who should have the major responsibility for the needs of the poor in the United States: the government or the poor themselves. More than three-quarters (76.9%) of the respondents indicate that government should have the major responsibility for the needs of poor people (see Table 46).

TABLE 46

Responsibility for Needs of Poor?	Number	Percent
government	40	76.9%
poor	9	17.3%
don't know	3	5.8%

Racial Discrimination in Purchasing Homes

Respondents were asked if they think that government should see to it that residents can purchase homes without racial or ethnic discrimination. More than half (52.8%) of respondents agree that government should see to it that residents can purchase homes without racial or ethnic discrimination, while slightly more than a third (37.7%) do not consider government responsible for guaranteeing equal access to housing (see Table 47).

TABLE 47

Purchase Homes w/o Discrimination?	Number	Percent
yes	28	52.8%
no	20	37.7%
don't know	5	9.4%

Police Protection

Respondents were asked to indicate how good a job the police do in protecting the lives and the property of the people in the neighborhood. Nearly all respondents (87.1%) feel that police are doing a very good or fairly good job (see Table 48).

73

TABLE 48

Job Police Do	Number	Percent
very good	7	13.0%
fairly good	40	74.1%
fairly poor	3	5.6%
poor	4	7.4%

Respondents were also asked if the Taunton police treat all citizens equally or if they give some people better treatment than they give others. More than seventy percent (71.2%) of respondents feel that the police in Taunton give some people better treatment than they give others (see Table 49). However, it is not clear whether perceptions of preferential treatment are related to a sense of ethnic discrimination, political favoritism, or socio-economic status.

TABLE 49

Police Treat Citizens Equally?	Number	Percent
equally	10	19.2%
some treated better	37	71.2%
don't know	5	9.6%

Summary and Conclusions

The survey found generally low levels of political and civic participation among Portuguese-Americans, but for u.s. citizens, these levels of participation are comparable to non-Portuguese groups across most variables: voter registration, working on political campaigns, contributing funds to political candidates or causes, levels of political information, interest in politics, discussions about politics, reading newspapers and magazines, watching television news broadcasts, listening to talk radio shows, contacting government officials, and membership in various civic organizations.

On the one hand, these results suggest that Portuguese-Americans are certainly no less likely to participate in politics and civic affairs than other Americans once they become U.S. citizens. The most noticeable differences are that Portuguese respondents express somewhat less interest in politics, obtain more of their political information from television as opposed to newspapers, and are less likely to contact a government official without an intermediary. On the other hand, these results also confirm the conventional wisdom that Portuguese-Americans do not participate in politics, have low levels of political knowledge, have high levels of distrust in government, and this is particularly true when non-citizens are included in the sample.

The results would seem to point to a three-pronged strategy for improving the rates of political and civic participation among Portuguese-Americans. First, since a disproportionate number of the non-U.S. citizens in this survey proved to be of Portuguese ancestry, it is clear that mobilization strategies should include citizenship training programs. Contrary to conventional wisdom, none of the respondents reported any expectation of "returning to the home country" as a reason for not becoming a citizen. The vast majority of non-citizens among the Portuguese expressed a desire to become a citizen, but most of these same persons saw their lack of English language and their lack of knowledge about how to become a citizen as the main obstacles to citizenship. This finding suggests that citizenship education programs should be continued, publicized, and targeted at persons of Portuguese ancestry in a bilingual format.

Once Portuguese-Americans become U.S. citizens, the evidence is clear that they participate and become involved in politics at least to the same extent as other Americans. Thus, a second strategy for mobilizing the Portuguese community must also focus on registering Portuguese-Americans to vote and then encouraging them to do so.

The United States is one of the few modern democracies that require voters to "register" prior to voting, although this process has become much easier in recent years. In general, it is well documented that persons are more likely to register to vote the easier the registration process. Registration is enhanced by passive mechanisms such as motor voter registration, frequent opportunities to register, information about how to register, assistance in registering, and elimination of literacy or language barriers. Significantly, Portuguese-Americans who report that they are not registered to vote indicate the main reason is lack of knowledge about how and where to register, as well as how to vote.

On many points, the survey results confirm the standard socio-economic model of political and civic participation, but one interesting finding of the survey was that educational attainment was more strongly correlated with levels of political and civic participation, and with levels of political knowledge, than any other variables examined in the study, such as income, occupation, gender, age, or ethnicity. There are several reasons why formal education exerts an influence on levels of political and civic participation as well as levels of political knowledge. Reading newspapers, filling out voter registration forms, following voter instructions, reading campaign literature, writing letters to public officials, and speaking in public are all manifestations of literacy, and in many ways voting mimics a form of "test-taking" for most individuals. The literacy skills acquired in formal education are readily transferable to the political sphere and, in many ways, they are crucial to many forms of political participation. A long-term strategy to increase levels of political and civic participation will include a number of activities aimed at increasing the general levels of formal educational attainment among Portuguese-Americans.

Finally, any strategy for mobilizing Portuguese-Americans must also build the community's civic organizations. Contrary to expectations, labor unions and the Catholic Church are not major sources of political information or civic involvement for most Portuguese-Americans. This is particularly surprising given the widely held assumption that both institutions are exceptionally influential among Portuguese-Americans due to occupational status and nearly universal identification (94%) with the Catholic religion. Yet, one of the remarkable peculiarities reported by Portuguese-Americans in the survey is that while they are more likely to make direct contact with government, they feel the need to act through intermediaries in the political process.

Consequently, citizenship and voter registration campaigns are fertile ground for non-partisan civic groups, including labor unions and the Catholic Church, to mobilize Portuguese-American voters. However, reported lack of knowledge about the basic mechanics of voting suggests that voter registration campaigns alone are insufficient, but need to be accompanied by more extensive voter and civic education programs. These programs should include information and instruction on how to register to vote, how to vote, sample ballots, where to vote, the use of punch cards and electronic voting machines. The programs should also include voter assistance on election day and more bilingual poll workers. There also needs to be a wider distribution of information about how to contact public officials at all levels of government, including names, addresses, and telephone numbers, as well as education about the availability of public officials to contact. The Portuguese language press is also a vital part of the Portuguese community's social capital, since survey respondents report that the Portuguese language media has a high rate of penetration within the Portuguese-American community. Nearly two-thirds of Portuguese-Americans in Taunton say they regularly receive information from some type of Portuguese language medium, including television, radio, and newspapers.

Moreover, the Portuguese-Americans surveyed for this study reveal a much stronger interest in local politics than in national or state politics, and other answers reveal a greater sense of political efficacy, responsiveness, and influence at the local level. It is difficult to know how much of this difference is explained by the existence of strong ethnic enclaves and political networks at the local level where Portuguese-Americans feel more comfortable and efficacious in the political process. It is also difficult to know how much of this difference is explained by the political content of the Portuguese language media, which may focus more on local issues (*O Jornal, Portuguese Times*) and international events (RPTI). It is not known how much of this interest may have been due to the presence of two prominent Portuguese-American elected officials in Taunton (Mayor Robert Nunes and State Senator Marc Pacheco). Nevertheless, it suggests that mobilization strategies are likely to be most effective when linked to "local" elections such as those for school committee, city council, mayor, and state legislator. Finally, a significant number of Portuguese-Americans report that they would like to become more involved in political and civic affairs, but again are unaware of how to go about volunteering to do political or civic work. The survey responses suggest that there is an untapped reservoir of political enthusiasm, but its mobilization will require initiative on the part of political and civic groups to find these persons and to bring them into the organized political process.

Notes

[1] The authors acknowledge the special assistance of Luis Dias, a former research assistant at the Center for Policy Analysis, who is currently a graduate student in public administration at Northeastern University.

[2] U.S. Census Bureau, *Census of Population and Housing, 1990.* (www.census.gov/)

[3] Robert S. Erikson, Norman L. Luttberg, and Kent L. Tedin, *American Public Opinion,* 4th Edition (New York: Macmillan Publishing Co., 1991), p. 123, observe that Verba and Nie's study remains "the most comprehensive study of political participation to date."

[4] Some Portuguese-Americans declined to participate in the survey because of language barriers. Bilingual survey interviewers were available, but many Portuguese speakers declined to participate in the survey, despite being called by a Portuguese-speaking interviewer. However, it is not possible to determine to what extent this factor plays a significant role in the survey results.

[5] Sidney Verba and Norman H. Nie, *Participation in America* (New York: Harper and Row, 1972), pp. 26-27.

[6] The 1990 Census reports that 11.3 percent of Census Tract 6137 are non-citizens and it is likely, given the census tract's demographic profile, that the vast majority of these non-citizens are of Portuguese ancestry. Thus, the telephone survey may have undersampled non-citizens, particularly non-English speakers, who often refused to participate in the survey despite the use of bilingual telephone interviewers.

[7] Massachusetts Secretary of the Commonwealth, "Massachusetts Registered Voter Enrollment, 1948-2000" (http://www.state.ma.us/sec/ele/eleenr/enridx.htm) reports 4,008,796 registered voters in Massachusetts in 2000. U.S. Census, "Profile of General Demographic Characteristics for Massachusetts, 2000," (http://www.census.gov/Press-Release/www/2001/tables/dp_ma_1990.PDF) show that Massachusetts had an approximate voting age population (age 18 and over) of 4,849,033. This means that approximately 87.5% of voting age residents who are U.S. citizens (4,582,361) in Massachusetts were registered to vote at the time of the survey.

[8] The respondents' self-reported voting in the 1996 U.S. Presidential election was overreported by respondents for reasons that are difficult to discern. In fact, only 56.3 precent of the state's voting age population turned out for this election. See, U.S. Census Bureau (1999, 301). One hypothesis is that respondents consider voting a basic civic responsibility and are therefore embarassed to admit to non-voting. Another possibility is that respondents are simply unable to differentiate between different elections.

[9] Respondents' self-reported voting in local elections is overreported by respondents for reasons that are difficult to discern. In fact, only 29.1 precent of Taunton's voting age population cast votes for the local state representative in the 1998 election (Tabulated from data in Massachusetts Secretary of the Commonwealth 1998).

[10] The 1990 Census reports that 11.3 percent of Census Tract 6137 residents are non-citizens and it is likely, given the census tract's demographic profile, that the vast majority of these non-citizens are of Portuguese ancestry. Thus, the key informant interviews oversampled non-citizens.

[11] In most U.S. voter behavior surveys, persons who are registered to vote, but who do not iden-

tify with a major political party are categorized as Independents. In Massachusetts, however, there is an Independent party listed on the voter registration form, so an individual who registers but does not identify with any political party is registered as "unenrolled" in a party.

[12]These percentages assume that non-respondents did not vote.

[13]These percentages assume that non-respondents did not vote.

[14]Erikson et al, *American Public Opinion,* p. 123.

[15]Erikson et al., *American Public Opinion,* pp. 79-81.

PORTUGUESE-AMERICANS IN SOUTHEASTERN MASSACHUSETTS: LEVELS OF POLITICAL EFFICACY

CLYDE W. BARROW

AND DAVID R. BORGES

There is a strong perception among all demographic groups in the United States that the political system does not adequately serve the interests of the public.[1] However, some groups feel more able to influence the actions of elected officials than others and this sensibility is called political efficacy. Political efficacy is the "belief that one can influence the political process. It is a feeling that an active citizen can play a part in bringing about social and political change, and that one's input counts."[2] Verba and Nie found that the higher the sense of political efficacy, the greater the likelihood that a person will participate in more demanding political activities. A low sense of political efficacy is usually correlated with political apathy and political alienation.[3]

This chapter compares the levels of political efficacy, political participation, political knowledge, and trust in government among Portuguese-Americans in Southeastern Massachusetts with other residents in the region. The survey includes many of the same questions that were asked in the Taunton, Massachusetts survey (Chapter 2), but the findings reported in this chapter are from a survey of the entire "Portuguese Archipelago" in Southeastern Massachusetts. The results for the larger Southeastern Massachusetts area are very similar to those reported for Taunton.

Survey Sample

There were 401 respondents to the survey. More than a quarter (28.6%) of the respondents identified themselves as Portuguese, Portuguese-American, or Cape Verdean. The majority of respondents (65.2%) were female. The average age of respondents is 45.0 years and they report a median family income between $25,000 and $45,000. Portuguese respondents have significantly lower levels of education in comparison to non-Portuguese. More than eighty-eight percent (88.4%) of non-Portuguese respondents have a high school diploma or GED, while 57.4 percent of Portuguese respondents have a high school diploma or GED. Almost a third (31.1%) of non-Portuguese respondents have a bachelor's or higher degree, while 14.9 percent of Portuguese-Americans have a bachelor's degree or higher (see Figure 1). A fifth of respondents (20.9%) primarily speak a language other than English (mainly Portuguese) and 13.3 percent were not born in the United States. Only 12.5 percent of the foreign-born respondents report that they have lived in the country for fewer than 10 years, while almost two-thirds of respondents (65.6%) report living in the United States for twenty years or more.

FIGURE I

Educational Attainment by Ethnicity

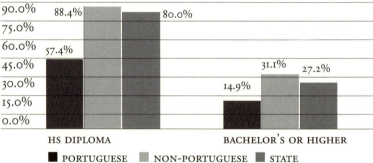

	HS DIPLOMA	BACHELOR'S OR HIGHER
PORTUGUESE	57.4%	14.9%
NON-PORTUGUESE	88.4%	31.1%
STATE	80.0%	27.2%

■ PORTUGUESE ■ NON-PORTUGUESE ■ STATE

Political Efficacy

The University of Michigan's National Election Studies have been used to calculate a Political Efficacy Index (PEI) for the United States since 1952, and the index consistently reveals that political efficacy is strongly associated with an individual's educational attainment, occupation, and income. In 1998, for example, the average PEI score for individuals with a high school diploma was 35. This compares to a PEI score of 42 for individuals with some college experience and a score of 59 for those with a college degree. Similarly, the average PEI score for individuals employed in professional occupations was 52 in 1998, compared to an index score of 33 for individuals employed in skilled blue collar occupations and 21 for those employed in unskilled occupations.[4] Portuguese-Americans in Southeastern Massachusetts generally have low levels of educational attainment and they are also disproportionately employed in blue-collar and unskilled occupations (see Chapter 4). The standard socio-economic model of political behavior therefore suggests that the region's Portuguese-Americans would also have a low sense of political efficacy.

Similarly, historical and cultural theories of ethnic political behavior point to the fact that Portugal and the Azores were governed by an authoritarian dictatorship from 1926 to 1974 when many of the Portuguese immigrated to Southeastern Massachusetts. Thus, it is often claimed that Portuguese immigrants do not have a history of political involvement and hence their sense of political efficacy is likely to be low in comparison to U.S citizens. Similarly, it is often claimed that life under an authoritarian dictatorship fostered high levels of distrust in government, which may also contribute to lower levels of political efficacy.

Political Influence

Respondents were asked several questions about their sense of political efficacy.

> *How much influence do you think people like you can have over state and local government - a lot, a moderate amount, some amount, or none at all?*

Only 9.2 percent of survey respondents feel that they have a lot of influence over state and local government, while 20.5 percent feel that they have no influence over state and local government (see Table 1). A higher percentage of Portuguese respondents (26.0%) feel that they have no influence over state and local government compared to non-Portuguese respondents (18.0%). Respondents who were not born in the United States, most of whom are Portuguese, are most likely to feel that they have no influence over state and local government.

TABLE 1

Influence Over State and Local Gov't	All Respondents Number/Percent		Portuguese Percent	Non-Portuguese Percent
a lot	35	9.2%	6.0%	10.3%
a moderate amount	98	25.8%	30.0%	24.6%
some amount	169	44.5%	38.0%	47.1%
none at all	78	20.5%	26.0%	18.0%

Most public officials (people in public office) are not really interested in the problems of the average person.

Nearly sixty-two percent (61.8%) of survey respondents strongly agree or somewhat agree with the statement that most public officials are not really interested in the problems of the average person (see Table 2). Only 12.7 percent of respondents strongly disagree with the statement. These results are consistent with the National Election Studies conducted in 1998, where 62.0 percent of respondents agreed with the statement that "public officials don't care what people think." Portuguese respondents (69.2%) are more likely than non-Portuguese respondents (59.5%) to strongly or somewhat agree that most public officials are not really interested in the problems of the average person.

TABLE 2

Public Officials Not Interested	All Respondents Number/Percent		Portuguese Percent	Non-Portuguese Percent
strongly agree	84	21.3%	24.3%	20.1%
somewhat agree	160	40.5%	44.9%	39.4%
somewhat disagree	101	25.6%	20.6%	27.2%
strongly disagree	50	12.7%	10.3%	13.3%

Citizenship, Voting, and Political Participation

Respondents were asked several questions about citizenship and voting. *Are you a U.S. Citizen?*

More than 95 percent (95.3%) of the survey respondents indicate that they are U.S. citizens (see Table 3). This compares to 94.5 percent of persons statewide who are U.S. citizens.[5] Of the 19 respondents who are not citizens, 15 (79%) are Portuguese.

TABLE 3

U.S. Citizen?	Number	Percent
Yes	382	95.3%
No	19	4.7%

Are you registered to vote?

Many studies have found a link between political efficacy and whether an individual votes.[6] Nearly ninety-percent of u.s. citizens (89.8%) in the survey report that they are registered to vote (see Table 4). This number is consistent with actual voter registration levels in Massachusetts, where approximately 87.5 percent of u.s. citizens were registered to vote at the time of the survey.[7] There is a small difference in the voter registration levels between Portuguese and non-Portuguese respondents, with 87.6 percent of Portuguese respondents (u.s. citizens) reporting they are registered to vote compared to 90.3 percent of non-Portuguese respondents.

When non-citizens are included in the sample, then 85.5 percent of the sample's total voting age population is registered to vote. This number is also consistent with actual voter registration levels in Massachusetts, where approximately 86 percent of the total voting age population was registered to vote at the time of the survey. The difference between Portuguese (77.6%) and non-Portuguese (84.1%) voter registration levels widens considerably when non-citizens are included in the sample.

A statistically significant relationship exists between education and voter registration. The percentage of respondents who are registered to vote increases as their educational levels increase (see Figure 2). The percentage of respondents who are registered to vote also increases with income level. This result is consistent with previous studies that confirm the standard socio-economic model.

TABLE 4

Registered to Vote	All Respondents Number/Percent		Portuguese Percent	Non-Portuguese Percent
Yes	343	89.8%	87.6%	90.3%
No	39	10.2%	12.4%	9.7%

FIGURE 2

Are You Registered to Vote

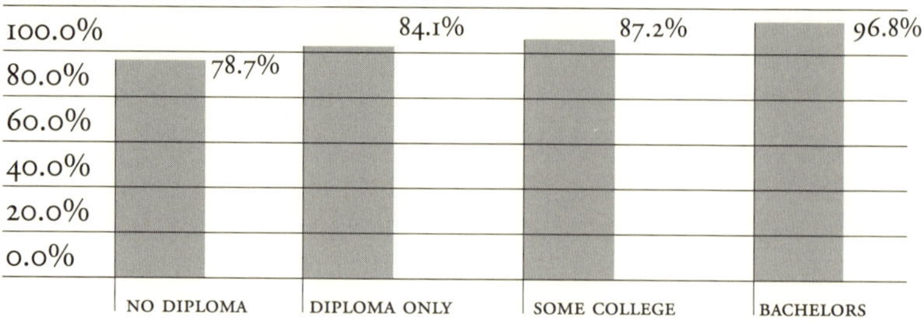

Voting in State and Local Elections

Do you always vote in state and local elections, do you sometimes miss one, or do you rarely vote, or do you never vote?

Individuals are more likely to vote when they have high levels of political efficacy, that is, when they feel that "my vote matters." However, as Americans become increasingly discouraged with the political process, lower levels of political efficacy have been associated with declining voter turnouts.

Survey respondents were asked how often they vote in state and local elections. In general, respondents claim to vote regularly. About forty percent (40.1%) of the respondents who are registered to vote indicate that they always vote in state and local elections, while almost half (47.4%) indicate that they sometimes miss a state or local election (see Table 5). Only 8.1% of the registered survey respondents indicate that they rarely vote in state and local elections, while 4.4% of respondents never vote.

There is a statistically significant difference between Portuguese and non-Portuguese respondents, with Portuguese respondents more likely to vote in state and local elections than non-Portuguese respondents. This finding is consistent with the higher levels of interest in local government among Portuguese-Americans reported in the Taunton survey (see Chapter 2). When non-citizens are included in the sample, then only about 34.4 percent of respondents "always vote" in state and local elections, which is consistent with statewide trends in off-year elections.[8] As expected, respondents with higher incomes are more likely to vote in state and local elections than respondents with lower incomes.

TABLE 5

How Often Do You Vote?	All Respondents Number/Percent		Portuguese Percent	Non-Portuguese Percent
always vote	138	40.1%	53.5%	35.6%
sometimes miss one	163	47.4%	32.6%	52.4%
rarely vote	28	8.1%	10.5%	7.6%
never vote	15	4.4%	3.5%	4.4%

How often do you attend City Council or Town Meetings in your city or town?

Individuals who are actively engaged in the political process are more likely to have stronger feelings of political efficacy. However, most survey respondents do not participate in local meetings. More than half of respondents (52.0%) never attend a city council or town meeting, while a quarter (25.5%) rarely attend (see Table 6). Less than a fifth of respondents (18.5%) always or sometimes attend city council or town meetings. There are only minor differences between the responses of Portuguese and non-Portuguese respondents.

TABLE 6

How Often Attend City Council/Town Meetings?	All Respondents Number/Percent		Portuguese Percent	Non-Portuguese Percent
always attend	16	4.0%	3.6%	4.3%
sometimes attend	74	18.5%	17.1%	18.9%
rarely attend	102	25.5%	22.5%	27.1%
never attend	208	52.0%	56.8%	49.6%

Trust and Confidence in Government

Respondents were asked several questions about their trust and confidence in government. Higher levels of trust and confidence in government are usually correlated with high levels of political efficacy.

How much trust and confidence do you have in our federal government in Washington when it comes to handling domestic problems?

Only 6.7 percent of respondents have a great deal of confidence in the federal government, although 45.9 percent of respondents have a fair amount of confidence in the federal government (see Table 7). There is a significant correlation between ethnicity and a respondent's trust and confidence in the federal government, with a higher percentage of Portuguese respondents (12.5%) reporting a great deal of confidence in the federal government in comparison to non-Portuguese respondents (4.7%).

TABLE 7

Trust and Confidence in Federal Government	All Respondents Number/Percent		Portuguese Percent	Non-Portuguese Percent
a great deal	26	6.7%	12.5%	4.7%
a fair amount	177	45.9%	49.0%	45.3%
not very much	145	37.6%	28.8%	40.9%
none at all	38	9.8%	9.6%	9.1%

How much trust and confidence do you have in our state government when it comes to handling domestic problems?

Only 7.7 percent of respondents have a great deal of confidence in the state government (Massachusetts), although more than half of respondents (50.8%) have a fair amount of confidence (see Table 8). There is a significant correlation between ethnicity and respondents' trust and confidence in the state government, with a higher percentage of Portuguese respondents (13.9%) reporting a great deal of confidence in the state government in comparison to non-Portuguese respondents (4.7%).

TABLE 8

Trust and Confidence in State Government	All Respondents Number/Percent		Portuguese Percent	Non-Portuguese Percent
a great deal	30	7.7%	13.9%	4.7%
a fair amount	198	50.8%	45.4%	53.1%
not very much	137	35.1%	34.3%	36.4%
none at all	25	6.4%	6.5%	5.8%

How much trust and confidence do you have in our local government when it comes to handling domestic problems?

In general, the survey respondents have more confidence in local government in comparison to the state and federal governments. Nineteen percent (19.0%) of respondents have a great deal of confidence in their local government and 52.2 percent of respondents have a fair amount of confidence (see Table 9).

TABLE 9

Trust and Confidence in Local Government	All Respondents Number/Percent		Portuguese Percent	Non-Portuguese Percent
a great deal	73	19.0%	20.8%	18.6%
a fair amount	201	52.2%	50.9%	52.6%
not very much	90	23.4%	23.6%	23.4%
none at all	21	5.5%	4.7%	5.5%

TABLE 10

Good Understanding of National Issues	All Respondents Number/Percent		Portuguese Percent	Non-Portuguese Percent
strongly agree	162	41.0%	40.4%	41.5%
somewhat agree	178	45.1%	42.2%	45.8%
somewhat disagree	37	9.4%	12.8%	8.3%
strongly disagree	18	4.6%	4.6%	4.3%

Political Knowledge

High levels of political efficacy are usually correlated with an individual's knowledge about political issues and political leaders.[9] Consequently, respondents were asked about important national and local issues and they were also asked if they could name the Governor of Massachusetts and their u.s. Senators. While respondents generally consider themselves to have a good understanding of important political issues, a high percentage are unable to name major political figures such as the Massachusetts Governor and the state's two u.s. Senators.

I feel that I have a pretty good understanding of the important national political issues such as health care, education, and gun control.
Over eighty-six percent (86.1%) of respondents strongly agree or somewhat agree that they have a good understanding of important national political issues (see Table 10). Only 4.6 percent of respondents

strongly disagree with the statement.

I feel that I have a pretty good understanding of the important state and local government issues such as public school funding and transportation.

A large majority of respondents (83.5%) strongly or somewhat agree that they have a good understanding of important state and local government issues (see Table 11). Only 4.6 percent of respondents strongly disagree with the statement.

TABLE 11

Good Understanding of State/Local Issues	All Respondents Number/Percent		Portuguese Percent	Non-Portuguese Percent
strongly agree	147	37.3%	35.2%	38.1%
somewhat agree	182	46.2%	49.1%	45.3%
somewhat disagree	47	11.9%	11.1%	12.2%
strongly disagree	18	4.6%	4.6%	4.3%

What is the name of the Governor of Massachusetts?

Respondents were asked if they could name the Governor of Massachusetts. More than a third of respondents (38.6%) could not name Paul Cellucci, who was Governor at the time, as the Governor of Massachusetts (see Table 12). Portuguese respondents are less likely to know the name of the Governor of Massachusetts than non-Portuguese respondents and the difference is significant. Respondents with higher levels of education are better able to name the Governor of Massachusetts as are respondents who primarily speak English, who were born in the United States, and those who have higher incomes and each of these associations is a significant correlation.

TABLE 12

Governor of Massachusetts	All Respondents Number/Percent		Portuguese Percent	Non-Portuguese Percent
correct response	245	61.4%	47.3%	67.0%
incorrect response	41	10.3%	13.4%	9.0%
don't know	113	28.3%	39.3%	24.0%

What is the name of the U.S. Senators from Massachusetts?
Respondents were asked if they could name the two U.S. Senators from Massachusetts. Just over a third (37.3%) of the respondents were able to name Edward Kennedy and John Kerry as the United States Senators from Massachusetts (see Table 13). Portuguese respondents are less likely to know the name of the state's two U.S. Senators than are non-Portuguese respondents and this is a significant difference. Respondents who primarily speak English, have higher levels of educational attainment, were born in the United States, and who have higher incomes are more likely to know the name of the U.S. Senators than are other respondents and these correlations are significant.

89

TABLE 13

U.S. Senators from Massachusetts	All Respondents Number/Percent		Portuguese Percent	Non-Portuguese Percent
correct response	149	37.3%	32.4%	39.3%
one correct response	143	35.8%	29.7%	38.6%
incorrect response	15	3.8%	4.5%	3.2%
don't know	92	23.1%	33.3%	18.9%

TABLE 14

Interest in Politics	All Respondents Number/Percent		Portuguese Percent	Non-Portuguese Percent
very interested	57	14.3%	15.5%	13.9%
somewhat interested	210	52.6%	45.5%	55.4%
somewhat uninterested	60	15.0%	13.6%	15.4%
not interested	72	18.0%	25.5%	15.4%

Interest in Politics

In general, how interested are you in politics?
Respondents were asked how interested they are in politics. Only 14.3 percent of respondents are very interested in politics, although 52.6 percent are somewhat interested (see Table 14). Eighteen percent of respondents are not interested in politics. A slightly higher percentage of Portuguese respondents (25.5%) indicate that they are not interested in politics compared to non-Portuguese respondents (15.4%).

Respondents who do not primarily speak English, the majority of whom are Portuguese, are the least interested in politics. Respondents with incomes below $25,000 and respondents who possess lower levels of educational attainment are also less interested in politics than other respondents and these results are statistically significant.

Political Leadership

Respondents were asked their views about several issues regarding political leadership. There are no statistically significant differences between the responses of Portuguese and non-Portuguese respondents.

Does a candidate's party have an effect on whether or not you would support him or her?

Respondents were asked if a candidate's party has an effect on whether or not they would support him or her in an election. Nearly 60 percent of respondents (59.6%) indicate that a candidate's party affiliation would not have an effect on their choice of candidates (see Table 15). There is only a small difference between Portuguese and non-Portuguese respondents.

TABLE 15

Does Candidate's Party Matter?	All Respondents Number Percent	Portuguese Percent	Non-Portuguese Percent
Yes	135 40.4%	42.0%	40.2%
No	199 59.6 %	58.0%	59.8%

TABLE 16

People Best Represented by Leaders from Own Racial/Ethic Background?	All Respondents Number Percent	Portuguese Percent	Non-Portuguese Percent
Yes	74 19.5%	21.1%	18.9%
No	306 80.5%	78.9%	81.1%

Do you feel that people are best represented in politics by leaders from their own racial or ethnic background, or does a leader's background not make much difference?

Fewer than a fifth of respondents (19.5%) agree that people are best represented in politics by leaders from their own racial or ethnic background (see Table 16). There are only slight differences between the answers of Portuguese and non-Portuguese respondents.

There is a large Portuguese population in Southeastern Massachusetts. Do you believe that Portuguese-Americans are well-represented in important institutions of the region such as government and business?
Nearly three-quarters of respondents (73.7%) feel that Portuguese-Americans are well-represented in important institutions of the region such as government and business (see Table 17). However, there are statistically significant correlations between ethnicity and respondents' answers to this question. A significantly lower percentage of Portuguese respondents feel that Portuguese-Americans are well-represented in important institutions of the region in comparison to non-Portuguese respondents, although nearly two-thirds of Portuguese respondents still agree that the Portuguese are well-represented in the region's important institutions.

91

TABLE 17

Portuguese-Americans Well Represented?	All Respondents Number	Percent	Portuguese Percent	Non-Portuguese Percent
Yes	249	73.7%	65.7%	76.8%
No	89	26.3%	34.3%	23.2%

Do you think that ethnic minorities in this country get more attention from government than they deserve, about the right amount of attention, or less attention than they deserve?
Respondents were asked if ethnic minorities in this country get more attention from government than they deserve, about the right amount of attention, or less attention than they deserve (see Table 18). Nearly 45 percent of respondents (44.7%) feel that ethnic minorities get about the right amount of attention from government. Respondents who are foreign-born are more likely to report that minorities get less attention from the government than they deserve, while respondents born in the United States are more likely to indicate that minorities get more attention than they deserve from government.

TABLE 18

Ethnic Minorities-Amount of Attention from Gov't.	All Respondents Number Percent		Portuguese Percent	Non-Portuguese Percent
more attention	100	27.0%	24.5%	27.2%
about the right amount	166	44.7%	42.9%	45.9%
less attention	105	28.3%	32.7%	26.9%

TABLE 19

Source of Political Information	All Respondents Number Percent		Portuguese Percent	Non-Portuguese Percent
television	342	85.3%	83.9%	86.8%
newspapers	309	77.1%	68.8%	81.1%
radio	178	44.4%	42.0%	45.4%
friends	159	39.7%	33.9%	42.9%
unions	35	8.7%	7.1%	9.6%
employer	32	8.0%	8.0%	8.2%
church/religious org.	32	8.0%	11.6%	6.4%
other	51	12.7%	9.8%	13.6%

Sources of Political Information

Where do you get your information about politics and government?

Respondents were asked where they get their information about politics and government. Respondents were offered seven choices and were allowed to give more than one response. Respondents are most likely to get their information about politics and government from television (85.3%) and newspapers (77.1%), although large percentages also receive information from radio (44.4%) and friends (39.7%) (see Table 19). Few respondents receive political information from employers, unions, or churches. Other sources include family, Internet, library, magazines, politicians, and school.

Non-Portuguese respondents are more likely to get their information from newspapers and this correlation is statistically significant. Respondents with lower incomes are also less likely to get their political information from newspapers. These findings are highly consistent with the results of the Taunton survey, where the same question was posed to survey respondents.

In general, how much trust and confidence do you have in the mass media—such as newspapers, TV, and radio—when it comes to reporting the news fully, accurately, and fairly?

Respondents were asked how much trust and confidence they have in the mass media. Only 14.0 percent of respondents have a great deal of trust in the media, while 47.8 percent of respondents indicate that they have a fair amount of trust (see Table 20). There is a statistically significant correlation between ethnicity and a respondent's trust and confidence in the media. Portuguese respondents (22.7%) are more likely to have a great deal of confidence in the mass media in comparison to non-Portuguese respondents (10.8%). Respondents who speak a language other than English and who were not born in the United States are also more likely to have a great deal of trust in the mass media in comparison to other respondents. Less educated respondents are also more likely to have a great deal of trust in the mass media, and these are all significant correlations.

While many respondents are skeptical about the media, they nevertheless indicate that television and newspapers are their primary source of political information. The level of skepticism about the media increases with educational attainment; yet it is the more educated that read newspapers at higher rates than respondents with lower levels of education.

93

TABLE 20

Trust in Mass Media	All Respondents		Portuguese	Non-Portuguese
	Number	Percent	Percent	Percent
a great deal	55	14.0%	22.7%	10.8%
a fair amount	188	47.8%	40.0%	50.9%
not very much	114	29.0%	27.3%	29.6%
none at all	36	9.2%	10.0%	8.7%

Summary and Conclusions

The findings of this survey of residents in Southeastern Massachusetts is consistent with the socio-economic model of political behavior. The results indicate that, like most Americans, the residents of Southeastern Massachusetts have low levels of political efficacy.

Only 34.0 percent of the survey's respondents feel that they have a lot or even a moderate amount of influence over state and local government, while a fifth of respondents (20.5%) feel that they have no influence over state and local government. Nearly 62 percent of the survey's respondents (61.8%) strongly agree or somewhat agree with the statement that most public officials are not really interested in the problems of the average person, while only 12.7 percent of the respondents strongly disagree with the statement.

The low sense of political efficacy is reinforced by low levels of trust and confidence in government. Only 6.7 percent of the survey's respondents have a great deal of confidence in the federal government when it comes to handling domestic problems. Similarly, only 7.7 percent of respondents have a great deal of confidence in the state government and 19.0 percent of respondents have a great deal of confidence in local government. While most respondents are involved in the political process through voting, the findings confirm that most respondents are "voting specialists" and do not participate in other forms of political activity. For example, more than half of respondents (52.0%) never attend a City Council or Town meeting in their community. Furthermore, a large percentage of respondents have low levels of political knowledge, which also tends to be correlated with a lower sense of political efficacy. More than a third of respondents (38.6%) could not name the Governor of Massachusetts, and only 37.3% were able to name the two United States Senators from Massachusetts. Respondents with higher levels of education, higher incomes, and English proficiency tend to be the most informed as judged by this basic measure, and these factors combine to reveal that Portuguese-Americans often have lower levels of political information than other residents and citizens.

Surprisingly, while many respondents do not even know the names of highly visible public officials, a majority consider themselves well-informed about national, state, and local issues. Over eighty-six percent of the survey's respondents (86.1%) strongly agree or somewhat agree that they have a good understanding of important national political issues and 83.5 percent state that they have a good understanding of important state and local issues. Furthermore, respondents who incorrectly identified these public officials are actually more likely to

strongly agree that they have a good understanding of important federal, state, and local issues in comparison to other respondents. Yet,
many of these same respondents are skeptical about the very media
(i.e., television and newspapers), that they identify as their primary
source of political information.

The survey found generally low levels of political efficacy among
Portuguese-Americans and, on this point, there are few differences
between Portuguese and non-Portuguese respondents. However,
Portuguese respondents do reveal some unique and somewhat paradoxical characteristics. Portuguese-Americans in Southeastern
Massachusetts do have slightly lower feelings of political efficacy, but
much of this difference is attributable to foreign-born Portuguese-
Americans. Portuguese-Americans are also less interested in politics,
particularly if they are not citizens and are therefore excluded from voting – the "easiest" and most frequent form of political activity. Yet,
despite low levels of political efficacy, Portuguese-Americans generally
have greater confidence in all levels of government than non-
Portuguese respondents, and this attitude is certainly consistent with
their economic liberalism (see Chapter 4). Portuguese-Americans also
tend to be more trusting of the mass media.

95

Notes

[1]Center for Policy Attitudes, *Expecting More Say: The American Public on Its Role in
Government Decision Making.* (Washington, DC, 1999).

[2]Erikson et al, *American Public Opinion*, p. 123.

[3]David C. Schwartz, *Political Alienation and Political Behavior* (Chicago: Aldine Publishing
Co., 1973); Robert S. Gilmore and Robert B. Lamb, *Political Alienation in Contemporary America*
(New York: St. Martin's Press, 1975); Kevin Chen, *Political Alienation and Voting Turnout in the
United States, 1960-1988* (San Francisco: Mellon Research University Press, 1992).

[4]National Election Studies, *National Election Studies 1952 – 1998*, Times-Series Studies.
University of Michigan.

[5]U.S. Census Bureau, *Census of Population and Housing, 1990.*

[6]Center for Policy Attitudes, *Expecting More Say: The American Public on Its Role in
Government Decision Making.*

[7]Massachusetts Secretary of the Commonwealth, "Massachusetts Registered Voter
Enrollment, 1948-2000" http://www.state.ma.us/sec/ele/eleenr/enridx.htm reports 4,008,796 registered voters in Massachusetts in 2000. U.S. Census, "Profile of General Demographic
Characteristics for Massachusetts, 2000," http://www.census.gov/Press-Release/www/2001/tables
/dp_ma_1990.PDF show that Massachusetts had an approximate voting age population (age 18 and
over) of 4,849,033. This means that approximately 87.5% of voting age residents who are U.S. citizens (4,582,361) in Massachusetts were registered to vote at the time of the survey.

[8]U.S. Department of Commerce, *Statistical Abstract of the United States, 1999*, p.303 reports
that 36.8 percent of the voting age population voted in Massachusetts in the 1998 election.

[9]Center for Policy Attitudes, *Expecting More Say: The American Public on Its Role in
Government Decision Making.*

PORTUGUESE-AMERICANS IN SOUTHEASTERN MASSACHUSETTS:
VIEWS ON THE ECONOMY AND RATES OF ECONOMIC
SATISFACTION

CLYDE W. BARROW, DAVID R. BORGES,
AND SHAWNA E. SWEENEY

This chapter reports the findings of a survey comparing the economic views and rates of economic satisfaction of Portuguese-Americans in Southeastern Massachusetts with those of non-Portuguese residents. The interest in this topic stems from the significant concentrations of Portuguese-Americans in Southeastern Massachusetts. More than one-third (35.7%) of Southeastern Massachusetts' residents are primarily of Portuguese ancestry. Approximately 48.5 percent of Fall River's residents, 43.1 percent of New Bedford's residents, and 39.8 percent of Dartmouth's residents claim Portuguese as their primary ancestry (U.S. Census 1990).

The first chapter of this work pointed out that Portuguese immigration to the United States occurred in three major waves (1850-1870, 1890-1910, and 1950-1980) that were related mainly to economic factors in Portugal. Thus, there has always been an important economic basis for Portuguese immigration to Southeastern Massachusetts and, as Portuguese immigrants arrived in the region, they became a mainstay of the workforce in many of the region's key industries, such as whaling, fishing, textiles, apparel, and other manufacturing sectors. The majority of the region's early Portuguese immigrants were Azorean men who worked on American whaling vessels.[1] Azorean migration to the region accelerated in the early 1900's and many of these immigrants found employment in the region's booming textile and apparel industries.[2] This same pattern of industrial and occupational segregation continued during the second big wave of Portuguese immigration, with many of the new arrivals taking jobs in the fishing, textile, and apparel industries.

In general, the Portuguese in Southeastern Massachusetts came to the region with little education and few skills.[3] Consequently, a significant number of Portuguese-Americans have worked in the types of low-skill occupations that traditionally provide an entry point into the Massachusetts labor force for poorly educated immigrants.[4] In 1990, for instance, nearly fifty percent (49.5%) of the Portuguese immigrants in Massachusetts worked in the manufacturing sector – especially textiles and apparel – while another 2.8 worked percent in the fishing industry (see Table 1).[5]

TABLE I

Percent Distribution by Industry of Employed Persons Over 16 in 1999

Industry	Mass. Portuguese Foreign Born	Mass. Portuguese Born in U.S.	Bristol County All Residents
Agriculture, forestry, & fisheries	2.8	1.6	1.6
Mining	0.1	0.1	0.1
Construction	8.0	6.5	6.4
Manufacturing, nondurable goods	26.3	8.6	10.7
Manufacturing, durable goods	23.2	11.5	14.7
Transportation	1.7	4.0	3.1
Communications & public utilities	0.7	2.4	2.6
Wholesale trade	2.6	4.1	4.5
Retail trade	12.5	19.9	17.5
Finance, insurance & real estate	3.8	6.6	5.6
Services	17.7	34.6	32.0

SOURCE: MULCAHEY, *Portuguese Spinner: An American Story.*

However, these industries have been adversely affected by the emergence of a "new economy" in Massachusetts, which has shifted the demand for labor toward more highly skilled occupations in financial services, professional services, and high-tech manufacturing.[6] Many of the region's traditional industries have also been negatively affected by trade liberalization, which has given low wage developing countries a cost advantage in labor-intensive industries such as apparel manufacturing. As a result, the industries where Portuguese immigrants tend to seek employment have been devastated by employment losses over the last fifteen to twenty years.

For a variety of reasons, the Southeastern Massachusetts economy suffered an acute employment shock from 1985 to 1993 that was largely related to the decline of manufacturing employment. In New Bedford, total employment declined 29.3 percent from 47,352 in 1985 to 36,628 in 1999. The erosion of New Bedford's manufacturing base accounts for a significant portion of the total employment decline. Between 1985 and 1999, manufacturing employment in New Bedford fell by 55.1 percent from 20,528 to 9,212. From 1990 to 1999, Fall River's manufacturing employment declined by 32 percent, while Taunton's manufacturing employment increased by only 3 percent during this same period.[7] Employment in New Bedford's fishing industry fell by more than 42 percent during the 1990s.[8] For more than a decade, Southeastern Massachusetts has struggled with the structural shocks of de-industrialization and there is no question that the economic disruption has disproportionately affected the Portuguese-Americans who work in these industries.[9]

The results of Southeastern Massachusetts' de-industrialization are straightforward. Median household income in New Bedford is only $20,677 (1995) compared to a statewide median household income of $38,574. New Bedford ranks as the 348th lowest income community among the 351 municipalities in Massachusetts. New Bedford's poverty rate is one of the highest in New England with 14.6 percent of the City's residents living below the official poverty level. Nearly 1 in 6 (17.0 percent) of New Bedford's residents live in subsidized public housing, while 17.1 percent of the city's residents receive some type of public assistance compared to the statewide average of 7.7 percent. The condition of residents in Fall River is almost identical to that of New Bedford, while the situation in Taunton is only slightly better.[10] Thus, low levels of education among Portuguese-Americans, and the fact that many are employed in low-skill or low-income jobs in declining industries, suggests the hypothesis that Portuguese-Americans in the region, especially the foreign-born, may have lower rates of satisfaction with the economy and more liberal views on economic issues.[11]

Survey Sample

There were 400 respondents to the survey with nearly thirty percent (29.5%) of the respondents identifying themselves as Portuguese, Portuguese-American, or Cape Verdean. The majority of respondents (63.8%) were female. The average age of respondents is 46.0 years and they report a median family income between $25,000 and $45,000. Nearly four-fifths (78.4%) of all respondents have a high school diploma, while 21.1 percent of all respondents have a bachelor's degree or higher. Portuguese respondents have significantly lower levels of education in comparison to non-Portuguese respondents. A fifth of respondents (20.2%) primarily speak a language other than English and 16.0 percent of respondents were not born in the United States. Less than 10 percent of respondents (8.1%) report that they have lived in the country for less than 10 years, while nearly two-thirds of respondents have lived in the United States for twenty years or more.

There are statistically significant correlations between respondents' ethnicity and educational attainment. For example, the average last grade completed by non-Portuguese respondents is 13.3 years. This compares to 11.3 years for Portuguese respondents. Over four-fifths (83.4%) of non-Portuguese respondents have a high school diploma or General Equivalency Diploma (GED), while 66.4 percent of Portuguese respondents have a high school diploma or GED (see Figure 1). The findings also reveal statistically significant differences in the income levels of Portuguese and non-Portuguese respondents with Portuguese respondents (36.8%) more likely than non-Portuguese respondents (28.8%) to have an income below $25,000.[12]

FIGURE 1

Educational Attainment by Ethnicity

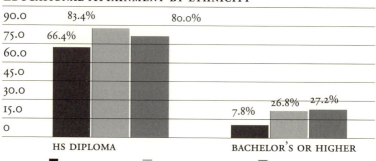

PORTUGUESE   NON-PORTUGUESE   STATE

Economic Issues

The survey respondents were asked to indicate their satisfaction with several aspects of the United States economy, economic issues, and economic policy. Residents were asked to rate their satisfaction on a scale of 1 to 4, with 1 being very unsatisfied, 2 being unsatisfied, 3 being satisfied, and 4 being very satisfied. A summary chart of the five issues is included at the end of this section (see Figure 2). Respondents are most satisfied with the state of the national economy and the opportunity for the next generation to live better than their parents. Respondents are more dissatisfied with the government's progress in reducing poverty and homelessness and the availability and affordability of health care.

How satisfied are you with . . .

The state of the nation's economy?
Nearly three-quarters of respondents (72.7%) are satisfied or very satisfied with the performance of the u.s. economy (see Table 2). This is not surprising since at the time of the survey, the United States was entering its ninth year of economic growth and unemployment rates were at a 30-year low both nationally and in Southeastern Massachusetts. Respondents with lower incomes express less satisfaction with the national economy in comparison to other respondents and this result is statistically significant. Respondents with a bachelor's degree or higher also express more satisfaction with the national economy in comparison to other respondents and this result is also statistically significant.

TABLE 2

Nation's Economy	All Respondents Number/Percent		Portuguese Percent	Non-Portuguese Percent
very satisfied	87	22.1%	18.1%	24.0%
satisfied	199	50.6%	57.8%	47.9%
unsatisfied	85	21.6%	20.7%	22.1%
very unsatisfied	22	5.6%	3.4%	6.0%

....the opportunity for the next generation of Americans to live better than their parents?
Respondents were asked how satisfied they are with the opportunity for the next generation of Americans to live better than their parents. More than half of respondents (59.6%) are satisfied or very satisfied with the next generation's prospects (see Table 3). Portuguese respondents (65.7%) are more likely than non-Portuguese respondents (56.9%) to report that they are satisfied or very satisfied with the opportunity for the next generation to live better than their parents.

TABLE 3

Opportunity for Next Generation to Live Better Than Parents	All Respondents Number/Percent		Portuguese Percent	Non-Portuguese Percent
very satisfied	66	17.3%	18.0%	16.9%
satisfied	161	42.3%	47.7%	40.0%
unsatisfied	109	28.6%	19.8%	32.7%
very unsatisfied	45	11.8%	14.4%	10.4%

TABLE 4

Opportunity for Poor Person to Get Ahead by Working Hard	All Respondents Number/Percent		Portuguese Percent	Non-Portuguese Percent
very satisfied	43	11.2%	14.4%	9.8%
satisfied	139	36.1%	34.2%	37.1%
unsatisfied	133	34.5%	32.4%	35.6%
very unsatisfied	70	18.2%	18.9%	17.4%

....the opportunity for a poor person in this country to get ahead by working hard?
Respondents were asked how satisfied they are with the opportunity for a poor person in this country to get ahead by working hard. Less than half of respondents (47.3%) are satisfied or very satisfied on this point (see Table 4). There is not a notable difference between Portuguese and non-Portuguese respondents. Almost the same percentage of Portuguese respondents (48.6%) and non-Portuguese respondents (46.9%) report that they are satisfied or very satisfied with

the opportunity for a poor person to get ahead by working hard. Of course, this means that a majority of both Portuguese (51.4%) and non-Portuguese (53.1%) respondents are dissatisfied or very dissatisfied with the opportunity for a poor person to get ahead by hard work.

....progress in reducing poverty and homelessness?

Respondents were asked how satisfied they are with the progress in reducing poverty and homelessness in the United States. Less than a quarter of respondents (24.3%) are satisfied or very satisfied with the nation's progress on this issue (see Table 5). There are minor differences between Portuguese (28.8%) and non-Portuguese respondents (22.6%) concerning their satisfaction with progress in reducing poverty and homelessness. However, during a period of almost unprecedented economic prosperity, a large majority of both Portuguese (71.2%) and non-Portuguese (77.4%) respondents were dissatisfied or very dissatisfied with the nation's progress in reducing poverty and homelessness.

TABLE 5

Reducing Poverty and Homelessness	All Respondents Number/Percent		Portuguese Percent	Non-Portuguese Percent
very satisfied	7	1.8%	2.7%	1.5%
satisfied	87	22.5%	26.1%	21.1%
unsatisfied	195	50.4%	45.0%	52.3%
very unsatisfied	98	25.3%	26.1%	25.2%

TABLE 6

Quality of Public Education	All Respondents Number/Percent		Portuguese Percent	Non-Portuguese Percent
very satisfied	37	9.7%	13.5%	8.0%
satisfied	147	38.5%	36.0%	39.5%
unsatisfied	146	38.2%	38.7%	38.7%
very unsatisfied	52	13.6%	11.7%	13.8%

...the quality of public education?

Respondents were asked how satisfied they are with the quality of public education. Less than half of respondents (48.2%) are satisfied or very satisfied with the quality of public education (see Table 6). Of these respondents, nearly equal percentages of Portuguese respondents (49.5%) and non-Portuguese respondents (47.5%) report that they are satisfied or very satisfied with the quality of public education. Despite implementation of the Massachusetts Education Reform Act of 1993, and several billion dollars in additional education spending by the state, a majority of both Portuguese (50.5%) and non-Portuguese (52.5%) respondents are still dissatisfied or very dissatisfied with the quality of public education in Southeastern Massachusetts.

....the availability and affordability of health care?

Slightly less than a quarter of respondents (24.9%) are satisfied or very satisfied with the availability and affordability of health care (see Table 7). Portuguese respondents (31.6%) are more likely than non-Portuguese respondents (22.6%) to report that they are satisfied or very satisfied with the availability and affordability of health care. Surprisingly, respondents who do not have a high school diploma are most likely to be satisfied or very satisfied with the affordability of health care and this may be due to the availability of government sponsored Medicaid and Medicare for the poor and elderly. Notably, however, this also means that a large majority of both Portuguese (68.4%) and non-Portuguese (77.4%) respondents are dissatisfied or very dissatisfied with the availability and affordability of health care.

TABLE 7

Availability/Affordability of Health Care	All Respondents Number/Percent		Portuguese Percent	Non-Portuguese Percent
very satisfied	23	5.9%	7.0%	5.3%
satisfied	74	19.0%	24.6%	17.3%
unsatisfied	150	38.5%	33.3%	40.2%
very unsatisfied	143	36.7%	35.1%	37.2%

Current Economic Situation

Respondents were asked several questions about their current financial situation and standard of living. Overall, there are only minor differences in the views of Portuguese and non-Portuguese respondents.

....during the last few years, has your financial situation been getting better, worse, or has it stayed the same?

Respondents were asked if their financial situation has been getting better, worse, or if it has stayed the same in the last few years. Over two-fifths of respondents (41.7%) indicate that their financial situation is getting better (see Table 8). There is a statistically significant correlation between a respondent's income and their financial situation. Respondents with lower incomes are more likely to indicate that their financial situation is getting worse, while respondents with at least some college or who have a bachelor's degree or higher are more likely to indicate that their financial situation has been getting better. There are only minor differences between the responses of Portuguese and non-Portuguese respondents, but the findings suggest that the new economy in Massachusetts is not benefiting all groups equally. Educational attainment is a key predictor of whether individuals' financial situation has improved during the most recent period of economic growth (1992-2000).

105

FIGURE 2

ECONOMIC ISSUES SUMMARY

Percent Indicating Satisfied or Very Satisfied

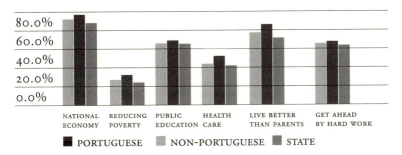

TABLE 8

Status of Financial Situation	All Respondents Number/Percent		Portuguese Percent	Non-Portuguese Percent
getting better	163	41.7%	42.1%	41.2%
getting worse	67	17.1%	16.7%	16.9%
stayed the same	161	41.2%	41.2%	41.9%

....compared to your parents when they were your age, do you think your own standard of living now is better, about the same, or worse than theirs was?

Respondents were asked if they think that their own standard of living now is better, about the same, or worse in comparison to their parents when they were their age. More than seventy percent (70.3%) of respondents agree that their financial situation is better than their parents was at their age (see Table 9). There are only minor differences between the responses of Portuguese and non-Portuguese respondents. Slightly fewer non-Portuguese respondents (69.9%) report that their standard of living now is better than their parents in comparison to Portuguese respondents (72.8%).

TABLE 9

Standard of Living Compared to Parents	All Respondents Number/Percent		Portuguese Percent	Non-Portuguese Percent
better	274	70.3%	72.8%	69.9%
worse	41	10.5%	19.3%	19.2%
about the same	75	19.2%	7.9%	10.9%

...in ten years, do you think that your standard of living will be better, worse, or about the same than it is now?

Respondents were asked if they believe that their standard of living will be better, worse, or about the same in ten years. More than half (57.3%) of respondents indicate that their standard of living will be better than it is now, although a third (32.6%) feel that it will be about the same (see Table 10). Almost two-fifths (38.9%) of the respondents who feel that their standard of living will be worse are age 55 to 64 and are likely to retire within ten years, which may suggest lingering concerns about the long-term viability of the U.S. Social Security and the

TABLE 10

Standard of Living in Ten Years	All Respondents Number/Percent		Portuguese Percent	Non-Portuguese Percent
better	199	57.3%	56.4%	57.7%
worse	35	10.1%	10.6%	9.8%
about the same	113	32.6%	33.0%	32.5%

TABLE 11

Having Political Connections	All Respondents Number/Percent		Portuguese Percent	Non-Portuguese Percent
very important	186	47.2%	50.0%	44.5%
somewhat important	112	28.4%	31.3%	28.3%
somewhat unimportant	71	18.0%	14.3%	20.2%
unimportant	25	6.3%	4.5%	7.0%

adequacy of private savings or company pensions. Respondents with lower incomes are more likely than other respondents to indicate that their financial situation will be worse in ten years and this result is statistically significant. There are only minor differences between the responses of Portuguese and non-Portuguese respondents.

Measures of Success

Respondents were read a list of items that are generally thought to help a person get ahead in life. Respondents were asked to rate the items on a scale from 1 to 4, with 1 being unimportant, 2 being somewhat unimportant, 3 being somewhat important, and 4 being very important in helping a person succeed. A summary chart of the five items is included at the end of this section (see Figure 3). While respondents rate all five of the measures fairly high, respondents are most likely to report that having a good education and hard work are important to succeed, while having wealthy parents and political connections are least important.

Having political connections or knowing the right people
Respondents were asked if having political connections or knowing the right people is important for a person to get ahead in life. Three-quarters of respondents (75.6%) agree that having connections is somewhat important or very important (see Table 11). Portuguese respondents (81.3%) are more likely than non-Portuguese respondents (72.8%) to report that having a connection is somewhat important or very important.[13] This finding is consistent with a recent survey of

employers in Southeastern Massachusetts, which found that 85 percent of the region's enterprises rely on company employees as their leading method of recruitment, which suggests that inter-personal networks and political connections remain an important aspect of the Southeastern Massachusetts economy.

Hard work and ambition

Almost nine-tenths (88.2%) of the respondents agree that hard work and ambition is somewhat important or very important to get ahead in life (see Table 12). There are only minor differences between Portuguese and non-Portuguese respondents on this issue, though a higher percentage of non-Portuguese respondents indicate that hard work and ambition is very important.

Having a good education

Nearly all respondents (94.2%) indicate that having a good education is somewhat important or very important (see Table 13). Portuguese respondents (86.2%) are more likely than non-Portuguese respondents (75.0%) to indicate that having a good education is very important.

Coming from a wealthy family

Respondents were asked if coming from a wealthy family is important for a person to get ahead in life. More than two-thirds of respondents (66.7%) agree that coming from a wealthy family is somewhat important or very important (see Table 14). Nearly the same percentages of Portuguese respondents (32.7%) and non-Portuguese respondents (31.6%) report that coming from a wealthy family is very important for a person to get ahead in life.

Having well-educated parents

Respondents were asked if having well-educated parents is important for a person to get ahead in life. More than three-quarters (79.4%) of respondents agree that having well educated parents is somewhat important or very important for a person to get ahead in life (see Table 15). A higher percentage of Portuguese respondents (44.8%) than non-Portuguese respondents (34.7%) report that having well-educated parents is very important.

TABLE 12

Hard Work and Ambition	All Respondents Number/Percent		Portuguese Percent	Non-Portuguese Percent
very important	217	54.7%	51.7%	57.2%
somewhat important	133	33.5%	36.2%	31.0%
somewhat unimportant	39	9.8%	10.3%	9.6%
unimportant	8	2.0%	1.7%	2.2%

TABLE 13

Having a Good Education	All Respondents Number/Percent		Portuguese Percent	Non-Portuguese Percent
very important	308	77.4%	86.2%	75.0%
somewhat important	67	16.8%	12.1%	18.4%
somewhat unimportant	17	4.3%	0.9%	4.8%
unimportant	6	1.5%	0.9%	1.8%

TABLE 14

Coming from a Wealthy Family	All Respondents Number/Percent		Portuguese Percent	Non-Portuguese Percent
very important	126	32.2%	32.7%	31.6%
somewhat important	135	34.5%	39.8%	32.7%
somewhat unimportant	96	24.6%	23.9%	25.3%
unimportant	34	8.7%	3.5%	10.4%

TABLE 15

Having Well-Educated Parents	All Respondents Number/Percent		Portuguese Percent	Non-Portuguese Percent
very important	149	37.8%	44.8%	34.7%
somewhat important	164	41.6%	36.2%	44.4%
somewhat unimportant	60	15.2%	17.2%	14.6%
unimportant	21	5.3%	1.7%	6.3%

Employment and Job Satisfaction

Respondents were asked about their employment status, where they worked, and several specific questions about their job. More than a third of respondents (37.5%) are employed full-time, while 25.8% are retired. Eighty-five percent (85.0%) of respondents are satisfied or very satisfied with their job. Nearly all respondents indicate that it is unlikely or fairly unlikely that they will lose their job or be laid off in the next year (93.0%).

What is your employment status?

More than a third of respondents (37.5%) are employed full-time, while 25.8 percent are retired (see Table 16). Portuguese respondents are more likely than non-Portuguese respondents to be employed full-time and are less likely to be retired.

What is your occupation?

Respondents were asked their occupation. The occupations are grouped by the United States Department of Labor employment categories. More than half of respondents (53.8%) are employed in white-collar occupations (see Table 17). A higher percentage of non-Portuguese respondents are employed in white collar jobs in comparison to Portuguese respondents.

TABLE 16

Employment Status	All Respondents Number/Percent		Portuguese Percent	Non-Portuguese Percent
employed full-time	150	37.5%	41.4%	37.0%
employed part-time	45	11.3%	12.9%	11.1%
self employed	17	4.3%	3.4%	4.8%
retired	103	25.8%	21.6%	27.0%
homemaker	35	8.8%	10.3%	8.1%
student	11	2.8%	0.0%	3.7%
unemployed-looking	20	5.0%	4.3%	5.2%
unemployed-not looking	15	3.8%	6.0%	3.0%

TABLE 17

Occupation	All Respondents	Portuguese Respondents	Non-Portuguese Respondents
WHITE COLLAR			
Executive/managerial	12.8%	12.5%	13.0%
Professional	19.7%	20.0%	19.5%
Technicians and related occ.	11.1%	5.0%	14.3%
Administrative Support	10.3%	10.0%	10.4%
Percent of Total:	53.9%	47.5%	57.2%
BLUE COLLAR			
Precision production, crafts, repair	6.0%	7.5%	5.2%
Machine operator/inspector /assembler	3.4%	7.5%	1.3%
Transportation/moving	4.3%	0.0%	6.5%
Handlers/helpers	1.7%	2.5%	1.3%
Percent of Total:	15.4%	17.5%	14.3%
SERVICE			
Service Occupations	30.7%	35.0%	28.6%
Percent of Total:	30.7%	35.0%	28.6%

FIGURE 3

MEASURE OF SUCCESS SUMMARY

Percent Indicating Important or Very Important

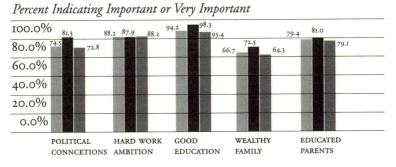

How satisfied are you with your job?

Respondents were asked to indicate their level of job satisfaction. More than four-fifths of respondents (85.0%) are satisfied or very satisfied with their job (see Table 18 and Figure 4). Portuguese respondents (54.4%) are more likely to be very satisfied with their job in comparison to non-Portuguese respondents (41.5%).

TABLE 18

Satisfaction w/Job	All Respondents Number/Percent		Portuguese Percent	Non-Portuguese Percent
very satisfied	97	45.8%	54.4%	41.5%
satisfied	83	39.2%	32.4%	42.3%
unsatisfied	19	9.0%	7.4%	9.9%
very unsatisfied	13	6.1%	5.9%	6.3%

FIGURE 4

How Satisfied Are You With Your Job?

VERY SATISFIED SATISFIED   UNSATISFIED   VERY UNSATISFIED

ALL RESPONDENTS   PORTUGUESE   NON-PORTUGUESE

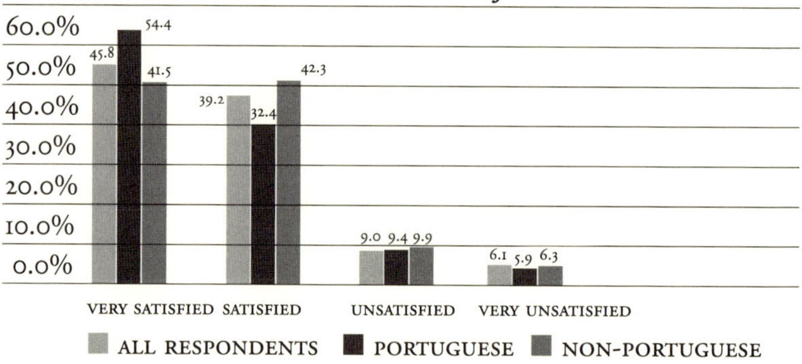

Satisfaction with Various Job Characteristics

Respondents were asked to rate their satisfaction with several job characteristics on a scale of 1 to 4, with 1 being very unsatisfied, 2 being unsatisfied, 3 being satisfied, and 4 being very satisfied. A summary chart of the seven categories is included at the end of this section (see Figure 5). Overall, respondents are most satisfied with their job security and the physical safety of the workplace, while they are least satisfied with their chance for promotion. There are no significant differences between the responses of Portuguese and non-Portuguese respondents.

There are also few differences with regard to a respondent's occupation, although respondents who work in the service sector are generally less likely to be very satisfied with different job characteristics than either white-collar professional or blue-collar manual workers.

Physical safety conditions of your workplace

More than four-fifths of respondents (82.2%) are satisfied or very satisfied with the physical safety conditions of their workplace (see Table 19). Again, there is only a minor difference between Portuguese (47.0%) and non-Portuguese respondents (51.4%) respondents and how they rate the physical safety conditions of their workplace.

TABLE 19

Physical Safety Conditions	All Respondents Number/Percent		Portuguese Percent	Non-Portuguese Percent
very satisfied	104	50.0%	47.0%	51.4%
satisfied	67	32.2%	36.4%	30.0%
unsatisfied	29	13.9%	12.1%	15.0%
very unsatisfied	8	3.8%	4.5%	3.6%

Your job security

Respondents were asked to rate their job security. More than eighty percent of respondents (82.5%) are satisfied or very satisfied with their current level of job security (see Table 20). Portuguese respondents (55.4%) are more likely than non-Portuguese respondents (47.5%) to be very satisfied with their job security.

TABLE 20

Job Security	All Respondents Number Percent		Portuguese Percent	Non-Portuguese Percent
very satisfied	103	50.0%	55.4%	47.5%
satisfied	67	32.5%	26.2%	35.3%
unsatisfied	23	11.2%	10.8%	11.5%
very unsatisfied	13	6.3%	7.7%	5.8%

Health insurance benefits your employer offers

Respondents were asked to rate their satisfaction with the health benefits that their employer offers. Nearly two-thirds of respondents (63.4%) are satisfied or very satisfied with the health insurance benefits that their company offers (see Table 21). Portuguese respondents (44.8%) are more likely than non-Portuguese respondents (34.7%) to be very satisfied with their health insurance benefits.

TABLE 21

Health Insurance Benefits	All Respondents Number/Percent		Portuguese Percent	Non-Portuguese Percent
very satisfied	68	37.8%	44.8%	34.7%
satisfied	46	25.6%	22.4%	26.4%
unsatisfied	29	16.1%	12.1%	18.2%
very unsatisfied	34	18.9%	20.7%	18.2%
does not offer	3	1.7%	0.0%	2.5%

Family and medical leave benefits your employer provides

Respondents were asked to rate their satisfaction with the family and medical leave benefits that their employer offers. Nearly two-thirds of respondents (65.5%) are satisfied or very satisfied with the family and medical leave benefits offered by their employer (see Table 22). Two-thirds of the non-Portuguese (66.6%) respondents report that they are satisfied or very satisfied with their family and medical leave benefits. Nearly equal percentages of Portuguese respondents (63.3%) report the same.

TABLE 22

Family and Medical Leave Benefits	All Respondents Number/Percent		Portuguese Percent	Non-Portuguese Percent
very satisfied	63	34.1%	35.0%	33.3%
satisfied	58	31.4%	28.3%	33.3%
unsatisfied	31	16.8%	16.7%	16.3%
very unsatisfied	32	17.3%	20.0%	16.3%
does not offer	1	0.5%	0.0%	0.8%

Your chance for promotion

Respondents were asked to rate their satisfaction with their chance for promotion. More than half of respondents (54.9%) are satisfied or very satisfied with their chance of promotion (see Table 23). Non-Portuguese respondents (23.8%) are more likely than Portuguese respondents (14.5%) to be very satisfied with their chance for a job promotion.

TABLE 23

Chance for Promotion	All Respondents Number/Percent		Portuguese Percent	Non-Portuguese Percent
very satisfied	39	21.0%	14.5%	23.8%
satisfied	63	33.9%	38.7%	32.0%
unsatisfied	39	21.0%	17.7%	22.1%
very unsatisfied	45	24.2%	29.0%	22.1%

TABLE 24

Retirement or Pension Plan	All Respondents Number/Percent		Portuguese Percent	Non-Portuguese Percent
very satisfied	53	31.9%	38.0%	29.8%
satisfied	56	33.7%	32.0%	34.2%
unsatisfied	29	17.5%	16.0%	18.4%
very unsatisfied	28	16.9%	14.0%	17.5%

TABLE 25

Money You Earn	All Respondents Number/Percent		Portuguese Percent	Non-Portuguese Percent
very satisfied	47	22.9%	18.2%	24.8%
satisfied	87	42.4%	45.5%	40.9%
unsatisfied	51	24.9%	30.3%	22.6%
very unsatisfied	20	9.8%	6.1%	11.7%

Retirement or pension plan your employer offers

Respondents were asked to rate their satisfaction with the retirement or pension plan that their company offers. Nearly two-thirds of respondents (65.6%) are satisfied or very satisfied with the retirement or pension plan that their company offers (see Table 24). Portuguese respondents (38.0%) are more likely than non-Portuguese respondents (29.8%) to be very satisfied with their retirement or pension plan.

Amount of money you earn

Respondents were asked to rate their satisfaction with the amount of money they earn. Nearly two-thirds of respondents (65.3%) are satisfied or very satisfied with the amount of money they earn (see Table 25). Again, a greater percentage of non-Portuguese respondents (24.8%) are more likely than Portuguese respondents (18.2%) to be very satisfied with the amount of money they earn at their current job.

How likely do you think it is that you will lose your job or be laid off in the next twelve months?

Respondents were asked how likely it is that they will lose your job or be laid off in the next twelve months (see Table 26). Nearly all of the respondents indicate that it is unlikely or fairly unlikely that they will lose their job or be laid off in the next year (93.0%). The sense of job security is high among both Portuguese and non-Portuguese respondents.

FIGURE 5

Job Characteristics Summary

Percent Indicating Satisfied or Very Satisfied

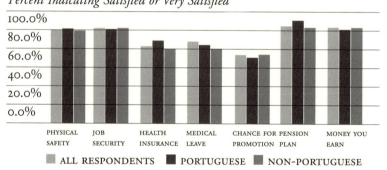

TABLE 26

Likelihood of Losing Job	All Respondents Number	Percent	Portuguese Percent	Non-Portuguese Percent
very likely	4	2.0%	3.1%	1.5%
fairly likely	10	5.0%	3.1%	6.0%
fairly unlikely	32	16.1%	20.3%	14.3%
not likely	153	76.9%	73.4%	78.2%

Do you own a home or rent?

Respondents were asked if they own their home. More than half of respondents own their home (60.5%). There are only slight differences in the percentages of Portuguese and non-Portuguese respondents who own and rent their home (see Table 27). Both groups are only slightly below the average rate of home ownership (61.7%) in Massachusetts.[14]

TABLE 27

Own or Rent Home	All Respondents Number/Percent		Portuguese Percent	Non-Portuguese Percent
own	240	60.5%	58.3%	61.0%
rent	131	33.0%	31.3%	34.6%
live w/parents	26	6.5%	10.4%	4.4%

Conclusions

The Portuguese-Americans who reside in Southeastern Massachusetts arrived with little education and few skills, but quickly became a mainstay of the fishing and manufacturing industries in Southeastern Massachusetts. They have a strong work ethic and believe that a good education and working hard is the key to personal economic success. A higher than average percentage of Portuguese-Americans work in blue-collar and service jobs that require lower levels of educational attainment and provide lower than average incomes. Nevertheless, they are generally satisfied with their economic progress over the last five years, have a better standard of living than their parents, and they are optimistic about the prospects for their children to be better off than themselves.

The vast majority of the region's Portuguese-Americans are satisfied with their jobs and, in a strong economy, there appears to be little concern about the prospect of unemployment, despite a massive wave of de-industrialization that swept the region less than a decade earlier. This suggests a great deal of resilience and the ability to quickly adapt to changing economic conditions, particularly their increased recognition of the importance of education in the new economy. Yet, the region's Portuguese-Americans are also concerned about the nation's lack of progress in reducing poverty and express doubts about the quality of public education, where most of their children attend school. They recognize that pockets of poverty and unemployment still exist and that public schools will need to improve to insure the optimistic expectations they have about their children's future.

While Portuguese-Americans in Southeastern Massachusetts report that they are generally satisfied with their job security and the physical safety of their workplaces, nearly half (46.7%) are not satisfied with their chance for promotion. While a large majority of Portuguese-Americans, like other Americans, are satisfied with their health care benefits, approximately one-third (32.8%) are not satisfied with their health care benefits. More than one-third (36.7%) are not satisfied with their current medical and family leave benefits. Nearly one-third (30.0%) are dissatisfied with their current pension benefits. While a majority is satisfied with their current earnings, more than a third of Portuguese-Americans (36.4%) are dissatisfied with their current earnings. There is a significant pocket of economic discontent within the Portuguese community, although it is one that mirrors the discontent of other working class residents, whose economic well-being depends on blue-collar jobs that are threatened by the combined forces of economic globalization, trade liberalization, the automation of manufacturing industries, and the shift to a new knowledge-intensive economy.

The survey results clearly indicate that these pockets of discontent are correlated with the respondents' level of education and income and to the extent that these factors bear disproportionately on Portuguese-Americans, they are of particular concern to the Portuguese community and its leadership. Not surprisingly, respondents with higher incomes and higher levels of educational attainment are more satisfied with the economy and their economic well-being than respondents with lower incomes and lower levels of education and this pattern holds for both Portuguese and non-Portuguese respondents.

As Marinho suggests in her essay (Chapter 7), historical culture and socio-economic status may converge to create these pockets of discontent as well as explain why most Portuguese-Americans are relatively satisfied with their situation despite working harder to achieve a moderate degree of economic success. Due to the lack of educational opportunities in Portugal and the Azores, Williams claims that Portuguese-Americans arrived in the United States with a culture that values hard work rather than education. This culture was reinforced by an Azorean economy based primarily on agriculture and fishing, where there were few good paying jobs and where seasonal unemployment was considered normal. Thus, it was necessary for most Portuguese families to have two working parents and a working extended family so the resources of the entire family could be pooled to support the household. As a result, children were encouraged to leave school at the earliest possible opportunity to seek employment.

Many Portuguese, especially those in the region's urban areas, continue to reside in ethnic neighborhoods where Portuguese is commonly spoken, where they have access to Portuguese language television, radio, and newspapers, and where they can find employment with little interaction outside their established ethnic boundaries. While these communities were important in helping new immigrants get established in America, it is often claimed that ethnic segregation has slowed their assimilation into American society and discouraged integration with the non-Portuguese community, including the loss of economic opportunities in new sectors of the economy. Because many Portuguese were slow to learn English and to adopt other aspects of American culture, including the high value placed on education, their upward mobility was slowed. Thus, Portuguese immigrants were able to succeed in Southeastern Massachusetts not through education or by creating ties to non-Portuguese social networks, but through hard work and by pooling the family resources as they had done in the Azores. However, to the extent that friends, ethnic networks, and political connections are still perceived as important to getting ahead in life, these networks, which are linked to the "old" manufacturing economy, may still channel Portuguese-Americans' opportunities for employment and promotion into declining sectors of the regional economy.

However, to the extent that this scenario is accurate, basic census data on household incomes, as well as that generated by our survey, could be somewhat misleading with respect to the economic situation of many Portuguese-Americans (see Table 28). The 1989 median household income of Portuguese immigrants ($32,500) is slightly higher than that of Portuguese-Americans born in the United States ($31,293) and it is on a par with the average income for all residents of Bristol County ($31,520).[15] Similarly, the 1990 U.S. Census reports that 8.9 percent of families in Massachusetts were below the federal (Census definition) poverty level. This compares to 8.9 percent of Portuguese-Americans families below the federal poverty level in Massachusetts, 13.3 percent in Fall River, and 14.6 percent in New Bedford.

Table 28

Median Household Income

Portuguese Immigrants	$32,500
Americans of Portuguese Ancestry	$31,293
All Bristol County Residents	$31,520
Massachusetts Residents	$32,952

Source: Mulcahy from *Portuguese Spinner, 278.*

However, if Williams' scenario is correct, the median *household* income of Portuguese-Americans, particularly the foreign-born, is primarily a result of the Portuguese having more workers in each household. Thus, while Portuguese households may appear to be doing as well economically as other households in the region, they may well be working harder to achieve the same level of success. Thus, it is certainly possible that the relative economic success of the Portuguese in Southeastern Massachusetts stems from the fact that in general, the Portuguese value hard work, spend less and save more, and pool the resources of the family rather than relying on one or two high-educated, high-income earners. Yet, it is this very work ethic that would lead many Portuguese-Americans to conclude that this is the normal path to economic prosperity even in a new economy that is rapidly shifting out from under the many Portuguese with low educational attainment and little job experience outside traditional manufacturing and fishing industries.

Notes

[1] Everett S. Allen, *Children of the Light: The Rise and Fall of New Bedford Whaling and the Death of the Artic Fleet* (Boston: Little, Brown, and Co., 1973).

[2] Jerry R. Williams, *And Yet They Come: Portuguese Immigration from the Azores to the United States* (New York: Center for Migration Studies, 1992); Aluisio Medeiros da Rosa Borges, *The Portuguese Working Class in the Durfee Mills of Fall River, Massachusetts: A Study of the Division of Labor, Ethnicity, and Labor Union Participation, 1895-1925* (Privately published, 1990); Philip T. Silvia, Jr., *The Spindle City: Labor, Politics, and Religion in Fall River, 1870-1905*, 2 Vols. (New York: P.T. Silvia, 1973).

[3] Until 1968, the Azores and mainland Portugal mandated only four years of formal education. See also, Toby E. Huff, Education and Ethnicity in Southeastern Massachusetts," *New England Board of Higher Education: Issues in Planning and Policymaking* (December 1989): 1-8.

[4] Andrew Sum and W. Neal Fogg, *The Changing Workforce: Immigrants and the New Economy in Massachusetts* (Boston: Massachusetts Institute for a New Commonwealth, 1999). For example, Clyde W. Barrow, *Economic Impacts of the Textiles and Apparel Industries in Massachusetts* (Boston: Donahue Institute and Center for Policy Analysis, 2000); Daniel Georgianna, *The Massachusetts Marine Economy* (Boston: Donahue Institute and Center for Policy Analysis, 2000).

[5] Maria Da Gloria Mulcahey, "Portuguese Spinner – An American Story," in Marsha McCabe and Joseph D. Thomas, eds., *Portuguese Spinner, 1998* (New Bedford, MA.: Spinner Publications, 1998), p. 276.

[6] United States International Trade Commission, *The Year in Trade: Operation of the Trade Agreements Program During 1997* (Washington, DC.: USITC Publication 3103, 1998); United States International Trade Commission, *Annual Statistical Report on U.S. Imports of Textiles and Apparel: 1997*, 3102 (Washington, DC: USITC Publication 3102, 1998).

[7] Calculated from Massachusetts Division of Employment and Training, "ES-202 Employment Data, 1985-1999," (Boston: DET Research Library).

[8] Calculated from Massachusetts Division of Employment and Training, "ES-202 Employment Data, 1985-1999," (Boston: DET Research Library).

[9] Cf. Barry Bluestone, *The Deindustrialization of America: Plant Closings, Community Abandonment, and the Dismantling of Basic Industries* (New York: Basic Books, 1982).

[10] See Clyde W. Barrow and David R. Borges, *Greater New Bedford Economic Base Analysis* (North Dartmouth, MA: Center for Policy Analysis and Greater New Bedford Workforce Investment Board, 2001).

[11] The term "liberal" is employed in its contemporary "American" usage, rather than its classical "European" usage, see, Kenneth M. Dolbeare and Linda J. Medcalf, *American Ideologies: Shaping the New Politics of the 1990s,* 2nd Edition (New York: McGraw-Hill, 1993), pp. 72-83, who describe this usage as an ideological orientation that seeks to promote social justice and equity through state action, while accepting the principle that such policies depend on the expansion and profitability of the private sector. This contrasts with "conservatives," who advocate a laissez-faire economic policy or socialists who advocate public and social ownership of the means of production.

[12] The findings should be interpreted with caution, because two variables often appear to be correlated, but are actually correlated with a third variable. For our sample, a partial correlation was run to partial out the effects of educational attainment on the correlation between income and ethnicity and vice versa. When we control for educational attainment, ethnicity loses its significance. However, when we control for ethnicity, educational attainment is still an important predictor of the income level of respondents in the sample. In other words, Portuguese-Americans' low level of educational attainment is a more important predictor of low income than ethnicity *ceteris paribus.* The results are consistent with the standard socioeconomic model, but they also point to the complex interrelation between class and ethnicity in the American social structure, see Bela Feldman-Bianco, "Multiple Layers of Time and Space: The (Re)Construction of Class, Ethnicity, and Nationalism Among Portuguese Immigrants." [Portuguese] *Revista Crítica de Ciências Sociais 38* (1993): 193-223.

[13] Steven Andrade, Clyde W. Barrow, and David R. Borges, *Strategies for Recruiting, Retaining and Training the Workforce of Tomorrow: A Blueprint for Action* (Boston: Donahue Institute and Greater Bristol Workforce Investment Board, 2001).

121

[14]U.S. *Census Bureau, Census of Population and Housing, 2000.* www.census.gov

[15]See, Williams, *And Yet They Come.* U.S. Census Bureau (1990) as reported in Mulcahy, *Portuguese Spinner,* p. 277. The U.S. Census Bureau's data on household income, includes all income earned from all sources by all persons living in a household. Consequently, it does not distinguish between a household earning $30,000 per year with one college educated worker and a household earning $30,000 per year with two workers lacking a high school diploma, nor does it differentiate whether income earners have more than one job.

PORTUGUESE-AMERICANS IN SOUTHEASTERN MASSACHUSETTS: OPINIONS ON SOCIAL AND CULTURAL ISSUES

CLYDE W. BARROW, SHAWNA E. SWEENEY,
AND DAVID R. BORGES

This chapter reports the results of a survey designed to measure the opinions of Portuguese-Americans in Southeastern Massachusetts on several controversial social and cultural issues in the United States. Survey research and public opinion theory draw a distinction between attitudes and opinions. An attitude is "a learned predisposition to respond consistently in a negative or positive fashion to an object in one's environment."[1] Since attitudes are mental states, they cannot be observed directly, but they can be inferred from behavioral indicators such as opinions, which are expressed verbally or in writing. Expressed opinions are never perfect indicators of attitudes, since a particular opinion may be driven by several conflicting underlying attitudes and thus opinions may fluctuate, even among the same group of people, depending on the intensity of the underlying attitudes or the way in which politics shifts a person's focus from one attitude to another. Thus, an individual may have a favorable attitude toward protecting the environment but express an opinion supporting the construction of a new school on wetlands because he or she also values education and considers it important to generate new construction jobs. Moreover, many survey research scholars argue that most of the American electorate does not have deeply held or intense attitudes, while low levels of political information make their opinions susceptible to change and volatility.[2] This chapter explores the opinions of Portuguese-Americans on issues such as education, immigration, abortion, homosexual unions, and educational and job opportunities for minorities and women.

It is widely claimed that the social and cultural attitudes of Portuguese-Americans are shaped by their religious beliefs, especially their connection to the Catholic Church. Nearly all of the Portuguese-Americans included in this survey express at least nominal adherence to the Catholic religion, and a number of Southeastern Massachusetts' most significant cultural activities consist of Portuguese religious feasts, such as the Feast of the Blessed Sacrament (New Bedford) and the New England Great Feast of the Holy Ghost (Fall River). The Catholic Church has often served as a center of Portuguese cultural life and has played a significant role in maintaining Portuguese cultural identity in their new country. This deep association with the Catholic Church might lead one to expect that Portuguese-Americans are inclined toward conservatism on social and cultural issues such as legalized abortion, homosexual unions, and other controversial social and cultural issues. This presumption is reinforced by the rural background of many Azoreans and Madeirans who immigrated to Southeastern Massachusetts, characteristically associated with more conservative social attitudes than urban residents.

Conventional wisdom also suggests that these attitudes, if present, would be retained and transmitted in the new country, since many of the Portuguese in Southeastern Massachusetts live in ethnic enclaves with well-developed social networks that assist them in finding housing and employment. Many Portuguese, especially those in the region's urban areas, continue to reside in ethnic neighborhoods where Portuguese is commonly spoken, where they have access to Portuguese language television, radio, and newspapers, and where they can find employment with little interaction outside their established ethnic boundaries. While these communities were important in helping new immigrants get established in America, some have argued that it slowed their assimilation into American society and discouraged their integration into the larger community.[3] These factors suggest the hypothesis that Portuguese-Americans in Southeastern Massachusetts should be more culturally and socially conservative than the u.s. population as a whole.

Survey Sample

There were 400 respondents to the survey, with a third (33.1%) of respondents identifying themselves as Portuguese, Portuguese-

American, or Cape Verdean. The majority of respondents (63.9%) were female. The average age of respondents is 48.0 years and they report a median family income between $25,000 and $45,000. More than four-fifths (81.7%) of the respondents have a high school diploma or GED, while 17.1 percent have a bachelor's degree or higher. Portuguese respondents have significantly lower levels of education compared to non-Portuguese respondents. Over ninety percent (90.4%) of non-Portuguese respondents have a high school diploma or GED, while 65.6 percent of Portuguese respondents have a high school diploma or GED (see Figure 1). Nearly twenty percent (19.9%) of non-Portuguese respondents have a bachelor's degree or higher, while only 8.0 percent of Portuguese respondents have a bachelor's degree or higher. More than a quarter (27.1%) of the respondents primarily speak a language other than English and 14.0 percent of respondents were not born in the United States.

FIGURE 1

EDUCATIONAL ATTAINMENT BY ETHNICITY

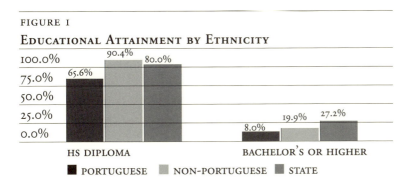

Education Issues

Respondents were asked several questions about education and prayer in public schools. The majority of respondents are very or somewhat satisfied with the quality of public schools in their city or town, feel that it is very important for a person to graduate college to be successful, agree that daily prayer should be allowed in the classroom, and support using public funds for religious or parochial schools.

How satisfied are you with the quality of the public schools in your city or town?

More than three-quarters of respondents (76.6%) are satisfied or somewhat satisfied with the quality of public schools in their city or town (see Table 1). There are only minor differences between the responses of Portuguese and non-Portuguese respondents on this issue. Respondents with higher levels of education are more likely to be very satisfied with the quality of public schools than are less educated respondents.[4]

TABLE 1

Quality of Public Schools	All Respondents Number/Percent		Portuguese Percent	Non-Portuguese Percent
very satisfied	75	24.0%	26.0%	22.7%
somewhat satisfied	164	52.6%	52.1%	53.0%
somewhat unsatisfied	31	9.9%	6.3%	12.6%
not satisfied	42	13.5%	15.6%	11.6%

How important is it for a person to graduate from college to become successful?

More than sixty-three percent of respondents (63.7%) feel that it is very important for a person to graduate from college to become successful (see Table 2). A majority of both Portuguese and non-Portuguese respondents agree that it is very important for a person to graduate from college.

TABLE 2

Graduating from College	All Respondents Number/Percent		Portuguese Percent	Non-Portuguese Percent
very important	249	63.7%	69.7%	60.2%
important	75	19.2%	16.4%	20.3%
somewhat important	52	13.3%	9.8%	15.9%
not important	15	3.8%	4.1%	3.6%

How do you feel about bilingual education?

A third of respondents are strongly in favor of bilingual education (33.8%), while 38.4 percent are somewhat in favor (see Table 3). In

1994, the National Election studies reported that nationally 28 percent of Americans were strongly in favor of bilingual education, while 40 percent of respondents were somewhat in favor, which suggests that Portuguese-Americans support bilingual education slightly more than the general public. There is a strong correlation between Portuguese ethnicity and support for bilingual education in our survey. A higher percentage of Portuguese respondents strongly favor bilingual education (54.1%) in comparison to non-Portuguese respondents (24.1%). Portuguese respondents who were not born in the United States are even more strongly in favor of bilingual education (73.8%) than u.s. born Portuguese respondents (44.3%).

TABLE 3

Bilingual Education	All Respondents Number/Percent		Portuguese Percent	Non-Portuguese Percent
strongly in favor	131	33.8%	54.1%	24.1%
somewhat in favor	149	38.4%	28.7%	42.9%
somewhat opposed	58	14.9%	5.7%	19.6%
strongly opposed	50	12.9%	11.5%	13.5%

TABLE 4

Daily Prayer in Classroom	All Respondents Number/Percent		Portuguese Percent	Non-Portuguese Percent
favor	245	65.0%	59.5%	68.0%
oppose	132	35.0%	40.5%	32.0%

Do you generally favor or oppose the following proposals concerning religion and public schools?

...allowing daily prayer to be spoken in the classroom

Nearly two-thirds of respondents (65.0%) favor allowing public prayer to be spoken in the classroom (see Table 4). This compares to 68.0 percent of Americans who agreed with this statement in a national Gallup poll taken shortly before the Southeastern Massachusetts survey (March 2000).[5] A majority of both Portuguese and non-Portuguese respondents favor allowing daily prayer to be spoken in public school classrooms.

...allowing public funds to be used in parochial or religious schools
Just over half of respondents (52.0%) favor allowing public funds to be used in parochial or religious schools (see Table 5 and Figure 2). A majority of both Portuguese and non-Portuguese respondents favor allowing public funds to be used for parochial schools. While a lower percentage of Portuguese respondents agree that daily prayer should be allowed in the classroom in comparison to non-Portuguese respondents, a higher percentage of Portuguese respondents favor using public funds for parochial or religious schools in comparison to non-Portuguese respondents.

128

TABLE 5

Public Funds for Parochial Schools	All Respondents Number Percent		Portuguese Percent	Non-Portuguese Percent
favor	191	52.0%	55.9%	51.9%
oppose	176	48.0%	44.1%	48.1%

FIGURE 2

RELIGION AND EDUCATION

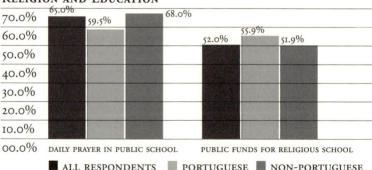

ALL RESPONDENTS PORTUGUESE NON-PORTUGUESE

Race and Ethnicity

Respondents were asked several questions about race and ethnicity. There are many differences between the responses of Portuguese and non-Portuguese respondents on these items. Portuguese respondents are more likely to think of themselves as a member of a particular ethnic, racial, or nationality group than are non-Portuguese respondents and they are also more likely to have felt discrimination because of their ethnicity. A higher percentage of Portuguese respondents also feel that racial and ethnic groups should maintain their distinct cultures than do non-Portuguese respondents.

When you think of social and cultural issues, do you think of yourself mainly as a member of a particular ethnic, racial, or nationality group, or do you think of yourself mainly as an American?

Only 10.7 percent of respondents think of themselves as a member of a particular ethnic, racial, or nationality group (see Table 6). A majority of both Portuguese (75.4%) and non-Portuguese (96.8%) respondents think of themselves mainly as an American. However, there is strong correlation between Portuguese ethnicity and ethnic identification. A higher percentage of Portuguese respondents think of themselves as a member of a particular ethnic, racial, or nationality group (24.6%) in comparison to non-Portuguese respondents (3.2%). Portuguese respondents who were not born in the United States are far more likely to think of themselves as members of a particular ethnic, racial, or nationality group (50.0%) than are Portuguese respondents who were born in the United States (12.7%).

TABLE 6

How Do You See Yourself?	All Respondents Number/Percent		Portuguese Percent	Non-Portuguese Percent
member of racial /ethnic group	41	10.7%	24.6%	3.2%
just an American	341	89.3%	75.4%	96.8%

TABLE 7

Discriminated Against?	All Respondents Number/Percent		Portuguese Percent	Non-Portuguese Percent
Yes	95	24.0%	32.0%	20.2%
No	301	76.0%	68.0%	79.8%

Have you ever felt any discrimination because of your ethnicity or race?

Twenty-four percent of respondents (24.0%) indicate that they have felt discrimination because of their ethnicity or race (see Table 7).

There is strong correlation between Portuguese ethnicity and feelings of discrimination. A higher percentage of Portuguese respondents (32.0%) report that they have felt discrimination because of their ethnicity or race in comparison to non-Portuguese respondents (20.2%). Portuguese respondents who were not born in the United States are far more likely to indicate that they have felt discrimination because of their ethnicity or race (41.9%) than are Portuguese respondents who were born in this country (27.2%).

Would you say that opportunities for a college education and jobs are, in general, better or worse, for racial or ethnic minorities than for non-minorities?

More than a third of respondents (37.4%) feel that opportunities for a college education and jobs are, in general, better for racial or ethnic minorities than for non-minorities, although 27.8% believe that the opportunities for minorities are worse (see Table 8). While there is not a notable difference between the responses of Portuguese-Americans and non-Portuguese respondents, more non-Portuguese respondents indicated that opportunities for a college education and jobs are worse for women than for men. This finding may reflect a long-standing cultural barrier to opportunities for women in the Portuguese community (see below).

TABLE 8

Opportunities for College and Jobs	All Respondents Number/Percent		Portuguese Percent	Non-Portuguese Percent
better	128	37.4%	35.5%	36.7%
worse	95	27.8%	33.6%	25.7%
same	119	34.8%	30.9%	37.6%

Do you think that it is better for America if different racial and ethnic groups maintain their distinct cultures or should groups change so that they blend into the larger society as in the idea of a melting pot?

More than sixty percent of respondents (60.9%) feel that racial and ethnic groups should change so that they blend into the larger society (see Table 9 and Figure 3). In 1996, the National Election Studies reported that 58.0 percent of respondents felt that racial and ethnic groups should change so that they blend into the larger society. There is strong correlation between Portuguese ethnicity and views on assimilation. A higher percentage of Portuguese respondents feel that racial and ethnic groups should maintain their distinct cultures (52.7%) in comparison to non-Portuguese respondents (31.2%). Portuguese respondents who were not born in the United States are far more likely to think that it is better for America if different racial and ethnic groups maintain their distinct cultures (70.3%) than are Portuguese respondents who were born in the United States (44.6%).

TABLE 9

Maintain Culture?	All Respondents Number/Percent		Portuguese Percent	Non-Portuguese Percent
maintain distinct cultures	135	39.1%	52.7%	31.2%
blend into the larger society	210	60.9%	47.3%	68.8%

FIGURE 3

Maintain Distinct Cultural or Blend into Larger Society?

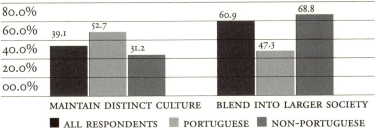

American Identity

Respondents were asked several questions to assess the importance they attach to various factors involved in being "truly American." Respondents are most likely to indicate that obtaining United States citizenship and being able to speak English are more important than having been born in America or having lived in the country for most of one's life, although the latter are still considered important by a majority of all groups. In general, there are only minor differences between the responses of Portuguese-American and non-Portuguese respondents.

How important do you think each of the following is for being truly American?

... To have been born in America

Just over half of respondents (52.5%) feel that it is very important or important to have been born in America to be truly American (see Table 10). In 1996, the National Election Studies reported that 68 percent of respondents felt that it was very important or important to have been born in America to be truly American. There are only minor differences between Portuguese and non-Portuguese respondents. There are also only minor differences between the responses of Portuguese who are foreign-born and Portuguese born in the United States.

TABLE 10

To Be Born in America	All Respondents Number Percent		Portuguese Percent	Non-Portuguese Percent
very important	115	29.3%	26.6%	31.2%
important	91	23.2%	25.8%	20.4%
somewhat important	85	21.7%	21.8%	22.8%
not important	101	25.8%	25.8%	25.6%

TABLE 11

To Be American Citizen	All Respondents Number Percent		Portuguese Percent	Non-Portuguese Percent
very important	273	69.6%	68.5%	70.7%
important	88	22.4%	25.0%	20.1%
somewhat important	10	2.6%	2.4%	2.8%
not important	21	5.4%	4.0%	6.4%

... To have American citizenship

A large majority of respondents (92.0%) feel that it is very important or important to have American citizenship to be truly American (see Table 11). In 1996, the National Election Studies also reported that 92.0 percent of respondents felt that it was very important or important to have American citizenship to be truly American. There are only small differences between Portuguese-American and non-Portuguese respondents. There are also only minor differences between the responses of foreign-born Portuguese and Portuguese born in the United States.

... To have lived in America for most of one's life

Sixty-three percent of respondents (63.0%) feel that it is very important or important to have lived in America for most of one's life to be truly American (see Table 12). In 1996, the National Election Studies reported that 73.0 percent of respondents felt that it was very important or important to have lived in America for most one's life to be truly American. There are only small differences between Portuguese-American and non-Portuguese respondents. There are also only minor differences between the responses of Portuguese who are foreign-born and Portuguese born in the United States.

133

TABLE 12

Lived in American for Most of Life	All Respondents Number/Percent		Portuguese Percent	Non-Portuguese Percent
very important	107	28.1%	28.3%	27.8%
important	133	34.9%	35.0%	34.7%
somewhat important	95	24.9%	24.2%	26.1%
not important	46	12.1%	12.5%	11.4%

... To be able to speak English

Nearly ninety percent of respondents (89.4%) feel that it is very important to speak English to be truly American (see Table 13). In 1996, the National Election Studies reported that 93.0 percent of respondents felt that it was very important or important to be able to speak English to be truly American. There are only small differences between Portuguese-American and non-Portuguese respondents. However, there is a statistically significant correlation between education and responses to this question. Respondents with lower levels of education indicate that being able to speak English is very important to be truly American than respondents with higher levels of education (see Figure 4).

TABLE 13

Able to Speak English	All Respondents Number/Percent		Portuguese Percent	Non-Portuguese Percent
very important	278	70.6%	72.0%	70.8%
important	74	18.8%	20.8%	16.8%
somewhat important	24	6.1%	2.4%	7.6%
not important	18	4.6%	4.8%	4.8%

FIGURE 4

How Important to be Truly American?

Percent Presponding "Very Important" or "Important"

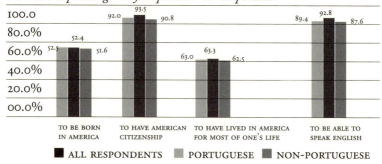

Language and Immigration Issues

Respondents were asked their opinions on several language and immigration issues being debated in the United States. Portuguese respondents are more likely than non-Portuguese respondents to oppose a law making English the official language of the United States, although a large majority of both groups favor such a law. Portuguese-Americans are also more likely to support an increase in immigration to the United States. Portuguese respondents are also more likely to agree that the United States should play a role in the reconstruction of East Timor.

Do you favor a law making English the official language of the United States, meaning government and business would be conducted in English only, or do you oppose such a law?

More than two-thirds of respondents (67.0%) favor a law making English the official language of the United States (see Table 14). A majority of Portuguese and non-Portuguese respondents support such a law. However, there is a strong correlation between Portuguese ethnicity and responses to this question. A lower percentage of Portuguese respondents (55.6%) favor making English the official language of the United States in comparison to non-Portuguese respondents (73.8%). Portuguese respondents who are foreign-born are the least likely to favor such a law (35.0%) in comparison to Portuguese respondents who were born in the United States (65.8%).

TABLE 14

EnglishOfficial Language?	*All Respondents Number/Percent*		*Portuguese Percent*	*Non-Portuguese Percent*
favor	250	67.0%	55.6%	73.8%
oppose	123	33.0%	44.4%	26.3%

TABLE 15

Level of Immigration	*All Respondents Number/Percent*		*Portuguese Percent*	*Non-Portuguese Percent*
increased a lot	16	4.5%	7.3%	3.0%
increased a little	34	9.5%	15.5%	6.5%
left the same	170	47.6%	40.9%	49.6%
decreased a little	74	20.7%	19.1%	22.8%
decreased a lot	63	17.6%	17.3%	18.1%

Do you think the number of immigrants from foreign countries who are permitted to come to the United States to live should be increased a lot, increased a little, left the same as it is now, decreased a little, or decreased a lot?

While nearly half of respondents (47.6%) feel that the number of immigrants from foreign countries should be left the same, 38.3 percent feel that the number of immigrants should be decreased a little or a lot (see Table 15). There is a statistically significant correlation between Portuguese ethnicity and responses to this question. A higher percentage of Portuguese respondents (22.8%) indicate that the number of immigrants should be increased a lot or a little in comparison to non-Portuguese respondents (9.5%), although this percentage is still lower than the percentage of Portuguese who would like to see the level of immigration decreased. Foreign-born Portuguese are more likely to support an increase in immigration than Portuguese respondents born in the United States and this difference is statistically significant.

Do you think the U.S. should play a key role in the reconstruction of East Timor as an independent country?

Nearly half of the survey respondents (47.0%) are not familiar with the East Timor issue (see Table 16). Portuguese respondents (43.1%) are almost as likely as non-Portuguese respondents (48.1%) to be unfamiliar with the issue.[6] Of those respondents who are familiar with the issue, 43.0 percent agree that the u.s. should play a key role in the reconstruction of East Timor. Portuguese respondents who are foreign-born are more likely to agree that the u.s. should play a key role in the reconstruction of East Timor (52.6%) than Portuguese respondents born in the United States (19.5%) and this difference is statistically significant. Foreign-born Portuguese are also more likely to be familiar with the issue than other groups. Respondents with higher levels of education also are more likely to feel that the u.s. should play a key role in the reconstruction of East Timor.

TABLE 16

Should U.S. Play Role in East Timor?	All Respondents Number/Percent		Portuguese Percent	Non-Portuguese Percent
yes	84	22.7%	30.2%	19.4%
no	112	30.3%	26.7%	32.5%
not familiar with issue	174	47.0%	43.1%	48.1%

Do you think that legal aliens who commit a felony should be deported?

More than sixty percent of respondents (63.9%) agree that legal aliens who commit a felony should be deported (see Table 17). A majority of both Portuguese and non-Portuguese respondents agree that legal aliens who commit a felony should be deported. However, there is strong a correlation between Portuguese ethnicity and responses to this question. A lower percentage of Portuguese respondents (53.8%) agree that legal aliens who commit a felony should be deported in comparison to non-Portuguese respondents (69.2%). Foreign-born Portuguese are less likely to agree that legal aliens who commit a felony should be deported (25.6%) than Portuguese-Americans born in the United States (67.5%).

TABLE 17

Legal Aliens Deported?	All Respondents Number/Percent		Portuguese Percent	Non-Portuguese Percent
yes	230	63.9%	53.8%	69.2%
no	130	36.1%	46.2%	30.8%

TABLE 18

Husband's Job to Earn Money	All Respondents Number/Percent		Portuguese Percent	Non-Portuguese Percent
strongly agree	32	8.2%	13.7%	6.0%
somewhat agree	58	14.8%	15.3%	13.9%
somewhat disagree	88	22.4%	29.0%	18.7%
strongly disagree	214	54.6%	41.9%	61.4%

Opportunities for Women

Respondents were asked three questions about opportunities for women. In general, respondents are fairly liberal in their opinions on these issues, although Portuguese-American respondents tend to have a slightly more traditional view of women's roles.

A husband's job is to earn money; a wife's job is to look after the home and family.
Respondents were asked whether they agree or disagree with the statement that "a husband's job is to earn money; a wife's job is to look after the home and family." Only 23.0 percent of respondents strongly or somewhat agree with the statement (see Table 18). A majority of

both Portuguese and non-Portuguese respondents disagree with this statement. However, support for traditional roles is slightly stronger among Portuguese-Americans. More than a quarter (29.0%) of Portuguese-American respondents strongly or somewhat agree with the statement in comparison to one-fifth (19.9%) of non-Portuguese respondents and this difference is statistically significant. Foreign-born Portuguese are even more likely to strongly or somewhat agree with the statement (41.9%) than u.s.-born Portuguese (21.3%), whose agreement is closer to that of other u.s.-born groups. This difference is also statistically significant.

138

Would you say that opportunities for a college education are, in general, better, worse, or the same for women as for men?

More than two-thirds of respondents (67.3%) feel that opportunities for a college education are the same for women as for men (see Table 19). Both a majority of Portuguese and non-Portuguese respondents feel that opportunities for a college education are the same for women and men and there are only minor differences between the responses of the two groups. However, there is a statistically significant correlation between the answers given by foreign-born Portuguese and u.s.-born Portuguese, with a higher percentage of the foreign-born Portuguese indicating that college opportunities for men and women are the same (76.3%) as compared to u.s.-born Portuguese (61.5%). None of the foreign-born Portuguese respondents agree that college opportunities are better for women than for men, while 16.3 percent of u.s.-born Portuguese respondents agree that college opportunities are better for women than men.

TABLE 19

Opportunity for College Education	All Respondents Number	Percent	Portuguese Percent	Non-Portuguese Percent
better	49	13.0%	11.1%	13.6%
worse	74	19.7%	23.1%	18.2%
same	253	67.3%	65.8%	68.2%

Would you say that employment opportunities are in general, better, worse, or the same for women than for men?

Respondents are more likely to agree that employment opportunities are worse for women than for men in comparison to their responses about educational opportunities. Nearly 45.1 percent of respondents agree that employment opportunities for women are worse than for men, although 45.9 percent of respondents feel that employment opportunities for women are the same (see Table 20). There are no significant differences between the opinions expressed by Portuguese and non-Portuguese respondents.

TABLE 20

Employment Opportunities	All Respondents Number/Percent		Portuguese Percent	Non-Portuguese Percent
better	34	9.0%	10.9%	8.3%
worse	170	45.1%	44.5%	44.6%
same	173	45.9%	44.5%	47.1%

TABLE 21

Violence Children Exposed to in Media a Problem	All Respondents Number/Percent		Portuguese Percent	Non-Portuguese Percent
very serious	237	61.1%	65.6%	59.6%
moderately serious	118	30.4%	29.5%	30.0%
not too serious	23	5.9%	2.5%	8.0%
not serious at all	10	2.6%	2.4%	2.4%

Social Issues

Respondents were asked to express their opinions on four social issues: children's exposure to media violence, homosexual unions, capital punishment, and abortion. Portuguese respondents are more socially conservative in comparison to non-Portuguese respondents with regard to homosexual unions and abortion, with foreign-born Portuguese being more conservative on these two issues than u.s.-born Portuguese.

How serious a problem is the amount of violence that children are exposed to in terms of the movies and television shows that they watch?

More than 61 percent of respondents (61.1%) feel that the amount of violence children are exposed to in the movies and television shows they watch is very serious (see Table 21). Only 8.5 percent of respondents feel that violence is not too serious a problem or not a problem. A majority of both Portuguese and non-Portuguese respondents feel that the amount of violence children are exposed to by the media is very serious.

In general, do you think homosexuals should be allowed to enter into legal unions similar to a marriage?

Southeastern Massachusetts is more socially liberal with regard to homosexual unions than the nation as a whole. A majority of respondents (57.9%) feel that homosexuals should be allowed to enter into legal unions similar to a marriage (see Table 22 and Figure 5) compared to 34 percent who held this opinion in a nationwide Gallup poll (January, 2000).[7] However, less than a majority (48.6%) of Portuguese respondents feel that homosexuals should be allowed to enter legal unions similar to marriage, while nearly two-thirds of non-Portuguese respondents (62.8%) felt that such unions are acceptable and this difference is statistically significant. However, it is the foreign-born Portuguese (25.7%) who are least likely to agree that homosexuals should be allowed to enter legal unions, while a sizeable majority (60.0%) of u.s.-born Portuguese-Americans consider such unions acceptable, and this difference is also statistically significant.

TABLE 22

Legal Unions	All Respondents Number/Percent		Portuguese Percent	Non-Portuguese Percent
should be allowed	201	57.9%	48.6%	62.8%
should not be allowed	146	42.1%	51.4%	37.2%

Are you in favor of the death penalty for a person convicted of murder?

A majority (57.6%) of respondents are in favor of the death penalty for a person convicted of murder (see Table 23 and Figure 6) compared to 66.0 percent who favored the death penalty in a nationwide

Gallup poll (March, 2000).[8] A majority of both Portuguese-American and non-Portuguese respondents are in favor of the death penalty for a person convicted of murder. However, foreign-born Portuguese are less likely to support the death penalty (39.5%)[9] than u.s.-born Portuguese (62.3%) and this difference is statistically significant.

FIGURE 5
Homosexuals Should Be Allowed to Enter Into Legal Unions

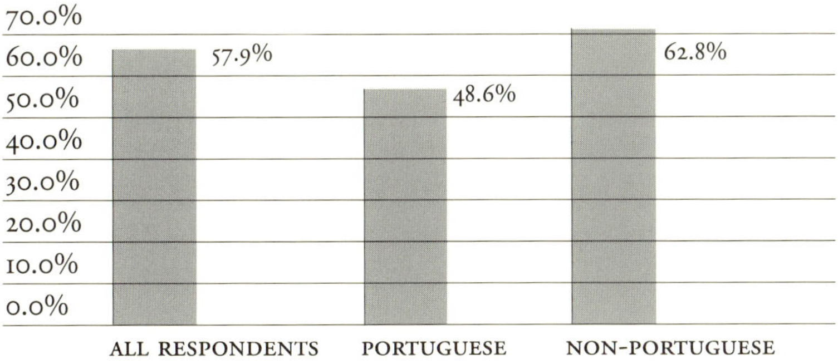

	ALL RESPONDENTS	PORTUGUESE	NON-PORTUGUESE
	57.9%	48.6%	62.8%

TABLE 23

Death Penalty	All Respondents Number/Percent		Portuguese Percent	Non-Portuguese Percent
yes	196	57.6%	54.6%	60.4%
no	144	42.4%	45.4%	39.6%

FIGURE 6
Support Death Penalty for Persons Convicted of Murder

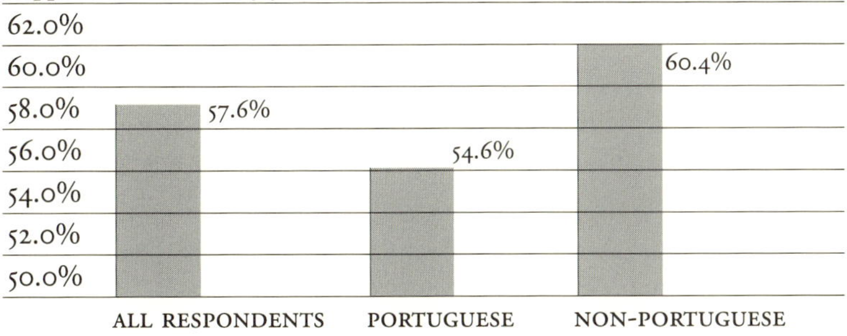

	ALL RESPONDENTS	PORTUGUESE	NON-PORTUGUESE
	57.6%	54.6%	60.4%

Do you think abortions should be legal under any circumstances, legal only under certain circumstances, or illegal in all circumstances?

The opinions of the persons surveyed in Southeastern Massachusetts mirror national results by the Gallup Poll. More than a quarter of respondents (27.5%) feel that abortions should be legal under any circumstances (see Table 24 and Figure 7) compared to 28.0 percent in a nationwide Gallup poll (March, 2000).[10] Nearly one-fifth (19.5%) of respondents feel that abortions should be illegal under all circumstances compared to 19.0 percent in a nationwide Gallup poll. There is a strong correlation between the responses of Portuguese-American and non-Portuguese respondents. A higher percentage of Portuguese respondents (28.6%) feel that abortion should be illegal under all circumstances compared to non-Portuguese respondents (14.9%), although 71.4 percent of Portuguese respondents feel that abortion should be legal even if restricted by circumstance. Foreign-born Portuguese are much more likely to agree that abortion should be illegal under all circumstances (48.8%) than u.s.-born Portuguese (17.3%) and this difference is statistically significant.[11]

TABLE 24

Abortion	All Respondents Number/Percent		Portuguese Percent	Non-Portuguese Percent
legal under any circumstances	103	27.5%	18.5%	32.0%
legal only under certain circumstances	198	52.9%	52.9%	53.1%
illegal in all circumstances	73	19.5%	28.6%	14.9%

FIGURE 7

Abortion

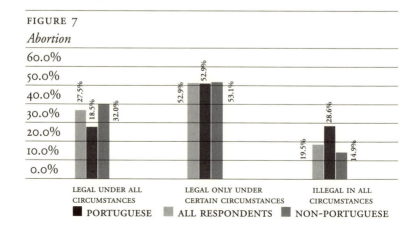

Summary and Conclusions

The opinions expressed by persons surveyed in Southeastern Massachusetts generally mirror those of the United States public as a whole. Nearly identical percentages of survey respondents in the regional and national surveys favor allowing public prayer to be spoken in the classroom, favor bilingual education, and feel that racial and ethnic groups should change so that they blend into the larger society. Similar percentages of respondents from the regional survey and national polls consider it important or very important to have American citizenship and to speak English to be "truly American." Similar percentages of respondents in the regional survey and national polls agree that abortions should be legal under any circumstances, while similar percentages also agree that abortions should be illegal under any circumstances. However, survey respondents in the Portuguese Archipelago are more likely than respondents nationally to agree that homosexuals should be allowed to enter legal unions similar to a marriage, while they are less likely to favor the death penalty for a person convicted of murder.

143

Within the Portuguese Archipelago, there are only minor differences between the opinions of Portuguese-American and non-Portuguese respondents on many issues. There are insignificant differences between Portuguese and non-Portuguese respondents on issues such as the quality of public education in their city or town, educational opportunities for ethnic minorities and women, the criteria for being "truly American," support for daily prayer in public school classrooms, concern over the level of violence that children are exposed to in the media, and support for the death penalty for convicted of murderers.

On other issues, however, there are statistically significant differences between the responses of Portuguese-American and non-Portuguese respondents. Portuguese-Americans are more likely to support bilingual education, to agree that immigration to the United States should be increased, and to uphold traditional roles for women. A higher percentage of Portuguese-Americans think of themselves as members of a particular ethnic, racial, or nationality group and a large number report that they have felt discriminated against because of their ethnicity. The Portuguese in Southeastern Massachusetts are also more likely than other groups to believe that racial and ethnic groups should maintain their distinct cultures. Similarly, a lower percentage of Portuguese-Americans favor making English the official language of the United States, agree that legal aliens who commit a felony should be deported, approve of homosexual unions, and believe that abortion should be legal under any circumstances.

Importantly, the statistically significant differences in the opinions of Portuguese-American and non-Portuguese respondents do not necessarily indicate the position of most Portuguese-Americans on these issues. In most cases, a majority of Portuguese-American and non-Portuguese respondents take similar positions on most issues, so the range of difference is mainly a matter of degree rather than due to deep-seated ideological or cultural differences. For example, a higher percentage of Portuguese respondents strongly or somewhat agree that a husband's job is to earn money while a wife's job is to look after the home and family, but a majority of both Portuguese-American and non-Portuguese respondents strongly or somewhat disagree with this statement. Similarly, a higher percentage of Portuguese respondents feel that abortion should be illegal under all circumstances in comparison to non-Portuguese respondents, but a majority of both groups agree that abortion should be legal under all or certain circumstances. There are also significant differences in social and cultural attitudes among the Portuguese, especially between foreign-born Portuguese and u.s.-born Portuguese. For example, Portuguese respondents who are foreign-born favor bilingual education more strongly, are more likely to think of themselves as members of a particular ethnic, racial, or nationality group, and are more likely to think it is better for America if different racial and ethnic groups maintain their distinct cultures. Foreign-born Portuguese are also less likely to favor a law making English the official language of the United States, more likely to support an increase in immigration, less likely to agree that legal aliens who commit a felony should be deported, and more likely to agree that abortion should be illegal under all circumstances.

In fact, if one excludes foreign-born Portuguese from the survey sample, there are only minor and infrequent differences between the opinions of Portuguese and non-Portuguese on most issues, which suggests that a great deal of assimilation takes place rather quickly among Portuguese-Americans. For example, it is the foreign-born Portuguese who are more likely than non-Portuguese respondents to support bilingual education, to think of themselves as members of a particular ethnic or racial group, to agree that different racial and ethnic groups should maintain their distinct culture, and to agree that a wife's job is to look after the home and the family. Indeed, many of the statistically significant differences that are noted between Portuguese-American and non-Portuguese respondents are attributable to the social and cultural attitudes of the foreign-born Portuguese.

Thus, the hypothesis proposed at the beginning of this chapter is partly true and partly false in two respects. First, the survey results suggest that it is necessary to refine this hypothesis in future studies by clearly delineating the analysis of social issues (i.e., individual and group rights) from cultural issues (i.e., moral values). The survey results show that the Portuguese are fairly liberal on social issues such as bilingual education, abortion, homosexual unions, and opportunity for women, although foreign-born Portuguese constitute a fairly conservative pocket within the larger Portuguese community on these issues. Second, Portuguese-Americans express many opinions that are best characterized as culturally conservative. The Portuguese are concerned about exposing children to excessive violence in the media, hold fairly traditional views of what it means to be "American," favor public funding for parochial schools and spoken prayer in public schools. Yet, on many of these issues, it is once again the foreign-born Portuguese who anchor this conservative tendency, while most u.s.-born Portuguese appear to adopt liberal views on most (but not all) cultural issues in the same proportions as Americans generally.

Notes

[1] Erikson et al., *American Public Opinion,* 4th edition, p. 44.

[2] Ibid., pp. 45-46.

[3] See, Williams, *And Yet They Come.*

[4] This result might seem to be in conflict with the findings in Chapter 4, where a majority of respondents stated they are dissatisfied or very dissatisfied "with the quality of public education." However, statewide and national surveys have consistently found that a majority of Americans claim they are dissatisfied with the quality of public education (when asked in the abstract), but satisfied with the quality of the public schools in their own town or city. This is a paradoxical finding given the below average performance of most public school systems in Southeastern Massachusetts, see David R. Borges and Clyde W. Barrow, *Fall River Public Schools Community Report Card, 2000* (North Dartmouth, Massachusetts: Center for Policy Analysis, 2001); Clyde W. Barrow, David R. Borges, and Paul Vigeant, *The SouthCoast Education Compact* (North Dartmouth, MA: SouthCoast

Chief Executive Officers, 1997).

[5]Gallup, www.gallup.com/poll/soc_issues.asp (2000).

[6]Peter Carey and G. Carter Bentley, eds., *East Timor at the Crossroads: The Forgin of a Nation* (Honolulu: University of Hawaii Press, 1995); Taro McGuinn, *East Timor: Island in Turmoil* (Minneapolis: Lerner Publications, 1998); Paul Hainsworth and Stephen McCloskey, eds., *The East Timor Question: The Struggle for Independence from Indonesia* (New York: I.B. Tauris, 2000).

[7]This question was worded slightly differently in each survey and thus the results are not strictly comparable, see Gallup, www.gallup.com/poll/soc_issues.asp (2000).

[8]Ibid.

[9]Portugal was one of the first countries to abolish the death penalty.

[10]Gallup, www.gallup.com/poll/soc_issues.asp (2000).

CHAPTER 6

PORTUGUESE LANGUAGE INSTRUCTION IN MASSACHUSETTS
PUBLIC SCHOOLS, COLLEGES, AND UNIVERSITIES

SHAWNA E. SWEENEY[1]

Since passage of the Massachusetts Education Reform Act of 1993, the state's Department of Education (MDOE) has adopted a number of "curriculum frameworks" that define objectives, content, and standards of instruction in the state's public schools.[2] The MDOE issued the first draft of its *Foreign Languages Curriculum Framework* for public comment in 1996 and it issued the final version of the curriculum framework in August of 1999. The *Foreign Languages Curriculum Framework* establishes mandatory statewide guidelines for learning, teaching, and assessment in modern foreign languages for the state's public schools. A core principle of the Massachusetts Foreign Languages Curriculum Framework is that all students enrolled in a public school should be able to read, write, and understand at least one language in addition to English at a high level of proficiency by the time they graduate from high school (grade 12). In addition, students of modern languages should be able to hold a conversation in the foreign language they are studying.[3] To achieve the goals of reading, writing, and conversing fluently in another language, the *Framework* recommends that students begin foreign language studies in the elementary grades and continue to study one or more languages through middle school and high school.

The *Foreign Languages Curriculum Framework* explicitly recognizes that national and state demographic characteristics are changing as a result of continued immigration and it requires that instruction be oriented towards the challenges posed by economic and political globalization. The *Framework* states that:

> as United States businesses expand domestic and international markets, their employees will benefit greatly from knowing another language. These skills

will allow them to obtain information directly from other countries, and to engage in face-to-face negotiations in political and business situations.[4]

The *Framework* emphasizes that more effective means of cross-cultural communication need to be developed in the public schools to facilitate linkages between local communities and the global community. One instructional method identified in the *Framework* to foster these linkages is to encourage students to use their "heritage language" in the classroom, in the home, and the local community. Heritage language speakers are students who have learned a language other than English in their homes. These students have varying proficiencies in their heritage language. Often they can have a fluent conversation, but require further instruction to sharpen other language skills such as reading, writing, and listening.[5]

In recent decades a large number of people have immigrated to the United States from Portugal, Cape Verde, Brazil, and other Lusophone nations. By 1975, immigrants from Portugal exceeded those from all other European countries.[6] In the Commonwealth of Massachusetts, there has been a significant immigration of Portuguese-speaking people over the last thirty years (see Chapter 1). Several Portuguese-speaking communities have been established in the state, particularly in the Southeast region.

Portuguese and other heritage language speakers will benefit from a rich and innovative curriculum where they can learn about the connections between their native language and other world cultures. They can participate in their local communities by performing songs and dances at local festivals. They can be active transmitters of their heritage language at the global level by traveling to other countries and interacting with native speakers, by learning about languages through innovative classroom projects, and by engaging in cross-cultural exchanges over the Internet.[7] With the advent of the Internet, students are able to engage in more active and spontaneous forms of communication with people from various cultures using different languages. In short, the high percentage of those who speak English as a second language, coupled with the immigration of people from Portugal and other Portuguese-speaking countries, suggests the importance of offering Portuguese language instruction in the state's public schools, par-

TABLE I

PORTUGUESE ANCESTRY OF 31 SELECTED COMMUNITIES

Municipality	Single Portuguese Ancestery Number/Percent		Primary Portuguese Ancestry Number/Percent		Single & Primary Portuguese Ancestry Number/Percent	
ACUSHNET	2,504	39.8%	618	19.8%	3,122	34.4%
BERKLEY	672	32.2%	309	16.2%	981	24.6%
DIGHTON	967	37.6%	329	12.5%	1,296	24.9%
DARTMOUTH	8,739	50.0%	1,530	14.9%	10,269	39.8%
EDGARTOWN	171	14.3%2	92	35.0%	263	11.6%
FAIRHAVEN	3,220	34.5%	1,418	30.6%	4,638	30.2%
FALL RIVER	37,737	55.8%	4,782	11.2%	42,519	48.5%
FALMOUTH	2,189	13.6%	599	6.1%	2,788	10.8%
FREETOWN	1,408	29.4%	519	26.9%	1,927	23.9%
GLOUCESTER	1,832	12.3%	997	8.6%	2,829	10.7%
HUDSON	2,225	23.2%	346	13.5%	2,571	16.0%
LUDLOW	4,294	34.7%	298	5.1%	4,592	25.3%
MARION	219	8.0%	92	29.6%	311	7.2%
MATTAPOISETT	567	18.7%	160	22.0%	727	12.8%
NEW BEDFORD	35,641	48.2%	5,023	12.4%	40,664	43.1%
OAK BLUFFS	297	18.0%	131	30.6%	428	16.1%
PEABODY	3,687	12.9%	457	11.0%	4,144	9.3%
PROVINCETOWN	993	46.5%	304	24.0%	1,297	38.1%
RAYNHAM	846	15.9%	369	8.9%	1,215	12.8%
REHOBOTH	889	22.2%	368	8.4%	1,257	15.0%
SEEKONK	1,415	20.5%	532	9.8%	1,947	15.8%
ROCHESTER	330	17.7%	128	27.9%	458	12.1%
SOMERSET	5,194	45.4%	931	15.2%	6,125	35.6%
SOMERVILLE	5,605	11.2%	600	2.8%	6,205	8.7%
STOUGHTON	2,396	15.6%	169	1.9%	2,565	10.5%
SWANSEA	3,123	33.7%	820	20.8%	3,943	26.9%
TAUNTON	12,289	38.9%	2,363	15.5%	14,652	31.3%
TISBURY	356	17.7%	140	28.2%	496	17.4%
TRURO	306	35.8%	141	21.8%	447	29.8%
WELLFLEET	160	11.6%	87	9.2%	247	10.7%
WESTPORT	3,403	39.4%	967	22.1%	4,370	33.2%
SOUTHCOAST	143,674	33.8%	25,619	15.1%	169,293	27.0%
MASSACHUSETTS	195,040	5.5%	46,133	19.1%	241,173	4.3%

SOURCE: U.S. CENSUS BUREAU 1990

ticularly in communities with a strong ethnic and linguistic link to Portugal, Brazil, and Cape Verde. Moreover, students of non-Portuguese heritage would be afforded the opportunity to learn about another language and other cultures in a setting where they can immerse themselves in the language spoken by members of their local community.

Methodology

Data was collected on foreign language instruction at the middle school and high school level for all Massachusetts towns and cities with a significant population of Portuguese-Americans. The purpose of the survey was to determine to what extent Portuguese language instruction is offered in those schools and whether students are given the opportunity to utilize their heritage language skills in the classroom. A town or city was classified as having a significant Portuguese population if 8 percent or more of its residents identified Portuguese as their primary ancestry in the 1990 *Census of Population.* There are 31 towns and cities in Massachusetts that meet this threshold. Table 1 provides a list of these towns and cities ranked by the percentage of the population that is of single and primary Portuguese ancestry.

A questionnaire was distributed to the foreign language or curriculum coordinator at the public schools in each of the identified towns and cities, requesting information on the types of languages offered at different grade levels, the number of teachers, student enrollments, and whether such courses are required or elective.[8] The Center for Policy Analysis also collected data on Portuguese language instruction at all colleges and universities in Massachusetts. The higher education data includes the level of instruction (lower-division, upper-division, graduate) at each college and university offering Portuguese language instruction, information on whether a major or a degree is offered in Portuguese language and culture and, where available, the number of students enrolled annually in Portuguese language and culture courses.

Middle and High Schools

Middle Schools

A major finding of the survey, particularly in light of the *Foreign Language Curriculum Framework's* commitment to heritage languages, is that Portuguese language instruction is not offered at the middle school level (grades 6-8) in the overwhelming majority of towns and cities where at least 8 percent of the population are of primary Portuguese ancestry. In fact, among the 30 survey respondents, the only communities that offer Portuguese language instruction at the middle school level are Fall River and Hudson. Fall River, which has the highest percentage of residents of Portuguese-American heritage, offers Portuguese for grades 6-8. Hudson also has a significant Portuguese population and reports offering Portuguese language instruction for grade 8. Other communities with a comparable percentage of Portuguese-American residents, including New Bedford, Dartmouth, Provincetown, Somerset, Westport, Acushnet, and Fairhaven did not report offering Portuguese language instruction at the middle school level, even though more than one-third of the residents in these communities are of Portuguese-American heritage.

At the same time, a significant number of courses are being offered in Spanish and French at the middle school level in most of these communities. The majority of the communities responding to the survey offer French and Spanish language instruction at one or all of the middle school grades. In several of these communities, between one-third and two-thirds of the student body are currently enrolled in French language instruction. In many of the same communities a significant percentage of students are enrolled in Spanish language courses. Table 2 briefly summarizes the data on language instruction for towns and cities with respect to French, Spanish, and Portuguese at the middle school level.

Secondary Schools
At the secondary school level (grades 9-12), a significantly higher number of towns and cities offer Portuguese language instruction. The following 17 communities offer Portuguese language instruction in high school:

• Dartmouth	Dighton	Fall River
• Falmouth	Freetown	Hudson
• Ludlow	Milford	New Bedford
• Rehoboth	Seekonk	Somerset
• Somerville	Stoughton	Swansea
• Taunton	Westport	

151

TABLE 2

PORTUGUESE-HERITAGE COMMUNITIES: FRENCH, SPANISH AND PORTUGUESE LANGUAGE INSTRUCTION AT THE MIDDLE SCHOOL LEVEL

Language	# of Communities
Spanish	22
French	21
Portuguese	2

Nevertheless, Spanish and French are still the most commonly offered foreign languages in high schools located in Portuguese-heritage communities. For the towns and cities where data were made available, 23 communities offer instruction in Spanish and French in grades 9-12 compared to 17 communities, which offer Portuguese. These communities are:

- Dartmouth
- Fall River
- Hudson
- Mattapoisett
- Raynham
- Seekonk
- Stoughton
- Wellfleet

Dighton
Falmouth
Ludlow
Milford
Rehoboth
Somerset
Swansea
Westport

Fairhaven
Freetown
New Bedford
Provincetown
Rochester
Somerville
Taunton

Table 3 provides a summary of the findings at the high school level. The table identifies the communities that offer instruction in Portuguese, French, and Spanish, the ratio of students enrolled in each language as a percentage of the total student enrollment, the percentage of the community that reports single and primary ancestries of Portuguese and French, and the percentage of persons in the community of Hispanic origin.[9]

These findings reveal that a majority of the communities offering Portuguese have a significant Portuguese population and that a significant percentage of the high school students in these communities are enrolled in Portuguese language courses. For instance, Fall River and

TABLE 3

Percentage of Students enrolled in Portuguese, French and Spanish for Selected Communities AY 1998-1999

Community	% Students enrolled in Portuguese (grades 9 - 12)	% Single & Primary Ancestry Portuguese	% Students enrolled in French (grades 9 - 12)	% Single & Primary Ancestry French	% Students enrolled in Spanish (grades 9 - 12)	% Persons of Hispanic Origin
Dartmouth	15.7%	39.8%	6.5%	11.3%	41%	0.7%
Dighton	13.4%	24.8%	8.6%	16.5%	41.4%	0.7%
Fairhaven	0%	30.2%	25.2%	22.1%	41.4%	0.7%
Fall River	27.4%	48.5%	9.8%	20.5%	22.7%	1.9%
Falmouth	5.4%	10.8%	13.8%	8.4%	35.1%	1.3%
Freetown	5.1%	23.9%	35.2%	22.1%	42%	0.1%
Hudson1	4.4	16.0%	11.3%	13.5%	25.3%	0.2%
Ludlow1	3.5%	25.3%	10.1%	23.6%	39.8%	2.0%
New Bedford	33.2%	43.1%	12.2%	15.5%	41.5%	5.6%
Mattapoisett*	0%	12.8%	19.8%	15.3%	66%	0.1%
Milford	5.2%	8.0%	10.6%	9.6%	46.2%	4.3%
Provincetown	0%	38.1%	25.5%	6.7%	39%	2.3%
Raynham	0%	12.8%	16.9%	14.4%	56.2%	0.9%
Rehoboth	13.4%	15%	8.6%	18.1%	41.4%	0.3%
Rochester*	0%	12.1%	19.8%	22.4%	66%	1.5%
Seekonk	16.8%	15.8%	13.2%	15.9%	12.4%	0.3%
Somerset	23%	35.6%	11.8%	21%	33.8%	1.5%
Somerville	5%	8.7%	34.5%	4.4%	55.8%	6.2%
Stoughton	6.6%	10.5%	16.6%	4.5%	41%	1.6%
Swansea**	26.9%**	24.5%*	0.7%			
Taunton	18.9%	31.3%	7.7%	13.5%	25.5%	4.5%
Wellfleet	0%	10.7%	21.5%	8.8%	42%	1.6%
Westport	21%	33.2%	7.2%	25.3%	23.2%	0.3%

* Numbers for the Old Rochester Regional School District, which includes the towns of Acushnet, Mattapoisett, Marion and Rochester, were combined.

** Swansea did not provide student enrollment figures for these foreign languages.

Source: U.S. Census 1990 & Massachusetts Department of Education, School and District Profiles 1998 - 1999institutions

153

New Bedford, which have the highest percentage of single and primary ancestry Portuguese-Americans (48.5% and 43.1%, respectively) and the highest percentage of primary and secondary ancestry Portuguese-Americans (52.9% and 47.8%, respectively), also have the highest percentage of students enrolled in Portuguese language courses. In the Town of Dartmouth, which has the 3rd highest percentage of single and primary ancestry (39.8%), and the 3rd highest percentage of primary and secondary ancestry (44.9%) Portuguese-Americans, 15.7 percent of the students enrolled in a foreign language course are taking Portuguese.

However, a number of communities with significant Portuguese-American populations do not offer the Portuguese language for grades 9 - 12. For example, 38.1 percent of the residents of Provincetown claim Portuguese as their single and primary ancestry and 42.9 percent claim Portuguese as their primary and secondary ancestry (4.8% secondary). Yet, instruction in the Portuguese language is not offered at either the middle school or the high school level. The Town of Fairhaven also has a significant Portuguese-American population and it does not offer Portuguese language instruction at either level.

Higher Education

As modern economies move toward information-, service- and technology-based industries, individuals without some level of post-secondary education will find it more difficult to compete in Massachusetts' new economy. Labor market projections by the U.S. Department of Labor and by non-profit research institutes predict that approximately 67 percent of all new jobs created in the future will require some level of post-secondary education such as a four-year college degree, a two-year community college degree, or certification by a technical institute.[10] In addition to enhancing career opportunities and earnings potential, a college education also plays a vital role in preparing students to participate actively in the political and social aspects of their communities.

According to a 1998 survey conducted by the Modern Language Association (MLA) on foreign language enrollments in U.S. colleges and universities, there has been a significant increase in registrations in several commonly taught languages. Although Spanish continues to be the most commonly taught foreign language in the United States,

Portuguese language instruction has also increased in higher education.

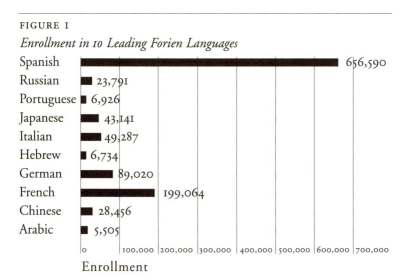

FIGURE I

Enrollment in 10 Leading Forien Languages

Spanish — 656,590
Russian — 23,791
Portuguese — 6,926
Japanese — 43,141
Italian — 49,287
Hebrew — 6,734
German — 89,020
French — 199,064
Chinese — 28,456
Arabic — 5,505

0   100,000 200,000 300,000 400,000 500,000 600,000 700,000

Enrollment

155

Table 4 shows the number of college and university students regis-tered nationwide in the ten leading modern foreign languages from 1970 to 1998.

TABLE 4

Registrations in 19 Leading Modern Foreign Languages, 1979 to 1998

	1970	1980	1990	1995	1998
Arabic	1,333	3,466	3,475	4,444	5,505
Chinese	6,238	11,366	19,490	26,471	28,456
French	359,313	248,361	272,472	205,351	199,064
German	202,569	126,910	133,348	96,263	89,020
Hebrew	16,567	19,429	12,995	7,479	6,734
Italian	34,244	34,791	49,699	43,760	49,287
Japanese	6,620	11,506	45,717	44,723	43,141
Portuguese	5,065	4,894	6,211	6,531	6,926
Russian	36,189	23,987	44,626	24,729	23,791
Spanish	389,150	379,379	533,944	606,286	656,590
Total	1,057,288	864,089	1,121,977	1,071,685	1,193,830

Source: Brod and Huber 1997, 4.

Figure 2 shows the change in the number of registrations for foreign language courses in colleges and universities from 1970 to 1998. The enrollment numbers reveal that between 1990 and 1995 registrations for Portuguese language courses increased by 5.2 percent, and between 1995 and 1998 registrations for Portuguese language courses increased by an additional 6.0 percent. This increase has occurred at a time when colleges and universities show declining enrollments in several foreign languages, most notably French and German. For example, between 1990 and 1995, registrations for French language instruction decreased by over 30 percent. Registration for French language courses continued to decrease between 1995 and 1998, but at a slower rate. Similarly, between 1990 and 1995 registrations for German language courses decreased by over 30 percent, and between 1995 and 1998 registrations for the language decreased by another 10 percent.

FIGURE 2

Changes in the Number
of Foreign Language Registrations
in Colleges and Universities, 1970 to 1998

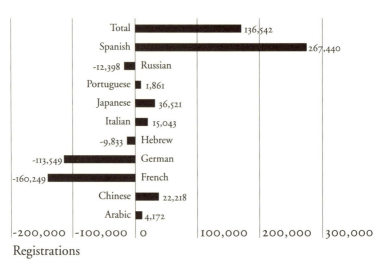

Data was collected on Portuguese language instruction at all colleges and universities in the Commonwealth of Massachusetts. A list of the institutions that offer Portuguese, the level of language instruction offered, the number of courses offered, and the type of degree offered are included in Table 5.

TABLE 5

MASSACHUSETTS COLLEGES AND UNIVERSITIES THAT OFFER PORTUGUESE LANGUAGE COURSES, AY 1999.

Name of Institution	# of Courses Offered & Level of Language Instruction	Type of Degree
Boston University	2 Elementary Courses & 2 Intermediate Courses	
Bridgewater State College	2 Elementary Courses & 2 Intermediate courses	
Bristol Com. Col.	2 Elementary Courses, 2 Intermediate Courses, 2 Conversation Courses, 1 Portuguese Literature Course, & 1 Brazilian Culture Course	
Bunkerhill Com. Col.	2 Elementary Courses	
Smith College	1 Elementary course *	
UMass-Amherst	3 Elementary Course, 4 Intermediate Courses & 17 Advanced Courses	Bachelor Master Doctorate
UMass-Boston	2 Elementary Courses, 2 Intermediate Courses & 7 Advanced Courses	
UMass-Dartmouth	4 Elementary Courses, 6 Intermediate Courses & 20 Advanced Courses	Bachelor
Westfield State College	3 Elementary Courses	
Harvard University	4 Elementary Courses 8 Intermediate Courses & 10 Advanced Courses	Bachelor Master Doctorate
Massasoit Com. Col.	2 Elementary Courses	
Middlesex Com. Col.	2 Elementary Courses	

157

The results indicate that there are few colleges and universities offering Portuguese language courses in Massachusetts. Only 12 (approximately 10%) of the 119 2-year and 4-year colleges and universities in the Commonwealth of Massachusetts offer Portuguese language instruction at the elementary, intermediate, and advanced levels. Only 3 offer a bachelor's degree and only 2 offer a graduate degree. Harvard University and the University of Massachusetts Amherst both offer a Master's degree and a Doctorate in Portuguese.

Notes

[1]The author acknowledges the special assistance of Diane Pimentel in collecting the data on public colleges and universities in Massachusetts.

[2]The Massachusetts Department of Education has issued seven curriculum frameworks in arts, English language, foreign languages, comprehensive health, mathematics, history and social science, and science and technology, see, http://www.doe.mass.edu/frameworks/

[3]Massachusetts Department of Education, *Foreign Languages Curriculum Framework* (Malden, Massachusetts, 1999), p. 9.

[4]Ibid., p. 59.

[5]Ibid., p. 28. Cf. U.S. Department of Labor, Teaching the SCANS Competencies (Washington, DC.: Secretary's Commission on Achieving Necessary Skills, 1993).

[6]Curriculum Research and Development Center, *The Need to Develop a System for the Assessment/Testing of Portuguese Speaking Students* (Kingston, RI: University of Rhode Island, 1977)

[7]Massachusetts Department of Education, *Foreign Language Curriculum Framework*, p. 59.

[8]The survey was originally faxed to all towns and cities on July 8, 1999. Telephone follow-ups were conducted on several dates between July 22nd and August 10th for towns and cities that failed to respond to the initial contact. After the follow-up calls, the survey was re-faxed on the following dates to the communities that still failed to respond: September 13th, 14th, and 28th; October 25th and 26th; and November 1st, 4th, and 8th. These efforts resulted in responses from thirty of the thirty-one towns and cities identified for the study.

[9]The enrollment data was obtained from the Foreign Language or Curriculum Coordinator in the school department of each town and city and from the Massachusetts Department of Education *School District Profiles*.

[10]William B. Johnston, *Workforce 2000: Work and Workers for the Twenty-First Century* (Indianapolis: Hudson Institute, 1987); George T. Silvestri and John M. Lukasiewicz, "Projections 2000: A Look at Occupational Employment Trends to the Year 2000," *Monthly Labor Review*, Vol. 110, no. 9 (September, 1987): 46-69.Commission on the Skills of the American Workforce, *America's Choice: High Skills or Low Wages!* (Rochester, N.Y.: National Center on Education and the Economy, 1990);

CHAPTER 7

PORTUGUESE-AMERICANS IN THE POLITICAL PROCESS:
A QUARTER CENTURY RETROSPECTIVE[1]

RITA DUARTE MARINHO

The political participation of Portuguese-Americans has commanded my intellectual interest since I was an undergraduate student at the University of Massachusetts Dartmouth. The topic's fascination for me has not diminished with the passage of time and, therefore, I am both flattered and excited to review the excellent studies conducted by the University of Massachusetts Dartmouth Center for Policy Analysis (CFPA). These studies address the question of civic and political partic-ipation, as well as political efficacy, among Portuguese-Americans in Southeastern Massachusetts generally and, more specifically, in a desig-nated census tract in Taunton, Massachusetts.

My objective in reviewing these studies is to compare the trends outlined there with the conclusions reached in my own survey research into similar concepts in 1977.[2] My work was updated in the early 1990's for publication, but I will use the 1977 data to provide a maximum timeframe for comparison.[3] I will also make some recommendations based on those findings, since the purpose of conducting these studies was to assist in developing practical strategies to involve the Luso-American community more fully in the political and civic life of the communities where they comprise a large segment of the population. Although the locus of the surveys is different, the methodologies, assumptions, and measuring instruments are similar enough to support some generalizations and, to that extent, the surveys conducted at both points of the twenty-five year interval suggest a dramatic and focused political strategy. The research also provides a reference for determining what is irrelevant to such a strategy and what is based on speculation, conjecture, and ethnic legend.

A Brief Review

Two channels of theory ebb and flow in their significance and effect when trying to explain American political behavior. One stems from generic studies begun about 50 years ago. The work by Verba and Nie cited in the Center's Taunton study (see Chapter 2) is the same one used in my own work, and though published in 1972, nothing has come along to replace their work as the standard for measuring American political behavior.[4] It should be noted, however, that Verba and Nie never intended to focus on ethnicity and its effect, if any, on political behavior.

A second body of work that originated in sociology and then migrated into political science focuses more directly on the effect of ethnicity on political behavior. Such studies typically examine specific ethnic groups and their machine politics – for example, Italians in New Haven, Poles in Chicago, Irish in Boston, Jews in New York, etc.[5] In terms of its theoretical linkage to the impact of ethnicity, this "socio-logical" body of work can be divided into three components. One group of studies, known as *cultural determinism*, attempts to use histor-ical experiences in the Old Country to predict or explain the behavior of a particular ethnic group in the United States.[6] A simple example would be using the historical conflict between the Irish and English to explain the high level of Irish-American political activity in the United States. A second component of this sociological literature is based on assimilation theory. Assimilation theory explains the political behavior of ethnic groups with sociological concepts such as *socio-economic sta-tus*, which includes education.[7] The basic idea, regardless of the partic-ular deployment of assimilation theory, is that as immigrants assimilate into American society they take on a variety of cultural and demo-graphic attributes that imbue them with a political stake in the system. The third component deals with the *structure* of American community and political institutions and how these structures help or hinder indi-viduals in their citizen activities.[8] For example, a Constitutional prohi-bition against aliens voting requires that individuals become citizens before they can vote. Local registration laws that require individuals to register every year or to pay a poll tax may preclude them from voting because they live too far away from the county seat in a centralized registration system or they cannot afford to pay the poll tax. Each component of this sociological literature offers various hypotheses about the effect of those factors they deem important, while most of the historical literature deploys just one theoretical framework. The development of a specifically focused theory helps us disentangle extremely complex political behavior, but when we attempt to engage in *applied* scholarship – that is building practical strategies to meet particular outcomes – it is usually a blend of theories that assists us best.

A Comparison

The political science literature has been very focused in its pursuit of questions pertaining to political behavior. Survey research (both academic and popular polling) has been arduously reinforcing its work for a half-century. It should come as no surprise that comparisons on the basis of similar questions can easily be made between my 1977 work on Portuguese-Americans and the studies presented in this collection.

Demographics

Most of the Portuguese-American community in Southeastern Massachusetts finds its roots in the Azores archipelago and most respondents profess the Catholic faith (over 95%). There has been no change in these ethnic characteristics between 1977 and 2000. The education statistics presented in the studies are particularly discouraging, because some of the 1977 data indicated an upward trend in the region's Portuguese-American educational attainment going back to the start of the century, but a comparison to the more recent survey data shows no change in educational attainment from 1977 to the present. Approximately 45 percent of the region's Portuguese-Americans still do not have a high school diploma. While the last grade achieved has moved from 9 to 10.6 during the last two decades, at this rate it would take another 50 years to achieve educational levels on a par with the American population at large. In the 1977 study, there was no difference in educational attainment between Portuguese whose families had immigrated before 1921 and those whose families had immigrated after 1965, which suggests that assimilation theory does not help in understanding why the Portuguese continue to drop out of school. Yet, even in 1977, seventy percent (70%) of the region's Portuguese-

Americans indicated that education was a necessary prerequisite to getting a good job. In short, the demographic picture of the Portuguese in Taunton in 2000 is quite similar to that described in the 1977 data for Portuguese in New Bedford and Providence. They come mostly from the Azores, they are Catholic, they are predominantly working-class, they stay put in their neighborhoods and tend to reside in enclaves, and they are undereducated as measured by formal education attainment.

Community and Political Life

There is much evidence to support the argument that sustaining democratic government requires the support and participation of informed citizens. This tradition is cogently argued as far back as Aristotle and continues to be supported by political scientists and journalists who analyze contemporary issues like the impact of television in Presidential campaigns. Two important citizen linkages are central to these arguments. First, the ability to sustain democracy as a system of government requires a participatory and informed citizenry. Second, political knowledge depends partly on formal educational attainment, but also on networks of political communication that establish different patterns of linkage between citizen and the political system. When one analyzes political communications networks, it is usually assumed that citizens are more likely to perceive a stake in the political community if they understand their own interests in the political system. It is really quite simple: if you do not know, you cannot care. If you do not care, you do not do anything about it.

Thus, there has been an abiding interest among political scientists in how immigrants to the United States receive information about their political and economic interests. The political communications loops have changed and evolved as technology has changed the methods of communication. Historically, citizens and ethnic groups received much of their political information through the political party structure. It was thought that this method was particularly influential for immigrants, who received political information in person (the most powerful form of communication) from an individual who could speak their language, which in turn decreased the potential for misunderstanding. As the party structure gave way to newspapers, then radio, and then television, it was hypothesized that impersonal modes of communication would have less effect on the individual, particularly on immigrants, who were now receiving political messages through impersonal means and, in many instances, not in their native language. What we have learned as political scientists during the past fifty years is that different media (i.e. the structures themselves) tell the political story differently as well.[9] People reading newspapers can appreciate more about context, gather more details, go back and reread a news story if they are puzzled by some question. Television requires both pictures and words and much shorter snippets of information – the sound bite.[10] Unless you are taping the television news, you cannot go back and rewatch it and there is much less room for details or context in a television news story.

163

Even in 1977, the Portuguese were watching more television as a source for information than reading newspapers. They have followed the national trend on this point, although television viewership among the region's Portuguese-Americans has increased in 2000, while newspaper readership has decreased from 75 percent to 59 percent. In 1977, cable was in its infancy as was the Portuguese Channel, so now there is more opportunity for the Portuguese to follow the news in their native language through television. And interestingly enough, the Portuguese believe themselves to be fairly well-informed on national and local issues. This is interesting data from a stake perspective, but it is wise to remember that issue voting is not compelling in American politics. Less than 10 percent of the American electorate votes solely on the basis of issues.[11]

When we turn to Portuguese-Americans' political information as measured by their ability to name office-holders, we find a dramatic decrease in the ability of the Portuguese to name the mayor or their representative in Congress. In 1977, 87 percent were able to name the mayor of their respective cities and 49 percent could name their representative in the u.s. Congress. In 2000, the number fell to 60 percent and 30 percent, respectively. It is difficult to assess why this decline in basic political knowledge has occurred over the last two decades. In 1977, neither the mayors nor Congressional representatives were Portuguese. Were the mayors more flamboyant in 1977? Is this important? Our natural instinct is to say: If people do not even know the name of the mayor, how in the world can they make an informed decision at the polls? This is a very basic piece of political information. Yet, unfortunately, the present low levels of political knowledge among the region's Portuguese is consistent with the American population in general.[12]

Another dimension to civic life that is considered important in the theoretical literature is the integration of citizens into community organizations as a precursor, adjunct, or parallel necessity to an engaged and vibrant political life. When we compare organizational activism between 1977 and 2000, an interesting pattern emerges over this time span. Union membership has decreased somewhat, but not by much, while church attendance has increased slightly. Membership in sports groups and nationality groups has increased dramatically, as has membership in community service organizations.

These increases have important implications for a fuller integration of the Portuguese into the political life of their communities. Membership and activism in community organizations produces a vision of a stake in the community, the so-called vested interest, which is supposed to give an impetus to voting. In addition, life in community organizations provides a crucial opportunity for apprenticeship as future political leaders, i.e. individuals who will run for or get appointed to public office. It is not only voting that is important; it is also a community's ability to produce a cadre of potential leaders for whom the Portuguese can vote.

Political Efficacy and Ideology

The CFPA studies also confirm the findings of my earlier survey research concerning political efficacy, cynicism and trust in government among Portuguese-Americans. The figures in the recent studies are almost identical to those in the earlier ones and the trends identified in the earlier studies remain intact in the current studies. Thus, the Portuguese continue to feel that they have little influence over government (only about 10% in both years believed that they had a lot of influence). However, the number of individuals who believe that officials are not much interested in the average person has increased from 40 percent to 61 percent. This change is possibly exaggerated as a result of using somewhat different questions in the two surveys, but it is also consistent with national trends among all groups in the United States.

The ideological questions are interesting to analyze in a comparative setting. The 1977 survey asked more specific questions to try to determine political ideology. In looking at both data sets, one can draw several conclusions. The Portuguese follow the same trend that has been identified for years by survey researchers. The more abstract the ideological questions, the more agreement; the more concrete the questions, the less agreement. The Portuguese with their tradition of strong family ties and enclave residency would be expected in the abstract to want to take care of the aged, infirm, and unemployed at home. During this same twenty-five years, one can safely assume that aggregate data analysis of those Portuguese participating in Medicare, Medicaid, unemployment compensation would parallel the population at large. That Portuguese tend to be more liberal than conservative on economic issues, an ideological position also demonstrated in 1977, should interest the Democratic Party in terms of numbers and the way candidates running for office might more readily appeal to the Portuguese community and its voters.

The connection between political efficacy and ethnicity was handled quite differently in the 1977 and 2000 surveys, and a form of the concrete/abstract dilemma may be associated with the 2000 survey conclusions. In 2000, the respondents were asked a series of questions, in the abstract, about their beliefs and values regarding whether a person of Portuguese heritage could better represent their interests. Twenty percent felt strongly that this attribute made a difference; 60 percent dismissed party affiliation as important; and 73 percent believe that Portuguese-Americans are well represented in important community and government institutions. In 1977, only 6 percent of respondents indicated that ethnic background, in the abstract, made a difference in their voting for a candidate.

In 1977, the surveys were all administered in person, while in 2000 these questions were part of a telephone survey. The 1977 study replicated a study that Pomper had conducted some years earlier, where a dummy ballot was handed to the respondent.[13] All the names were male and all were members of the Democratic Party. The names of the candidates reading from top to bottom were obviously Irish, Greek, Polish, French, Portuguese, English and Italian. Of those who voted, and most were willing, 83.5 percent selected the Portuguese name. This confirmed again that next to political party affiliation, ethnicity is the most important clue that voters use in identifying candidates who are friendlier to their point of view, absent any other kind of information, and regardless of what they state in the abstract.

Citizenship, Registration and Voting

One important change since the 1977 study is that more Portuguese appear to be u.s. citizens in 2000 than in 1977. In 1977, our sample indicated that 20 percent of Portuguese-Americans were not citizens, but were eligible to become citizens. Today's figure is 13.4 percent. It may be that the relentless policy enforcement of the Immigration and Naturalization Service (INS) and other eligibility requirements for federal social programs have had some unexpected returns in increasing American citizenship for Portuguese resident aliens. However, these particular issues were not explored in the current studies, which focused on why Portuguese-Americans *do not* become u.s. citizens. The reasons why they become u.s. citizens and the mechanisms that facilitate this process would be equally interesting for both academic and political purposes.

The comparison data regarding voter registration are also worth noting. In 1977, approximately 16 percent of eligible voters in Massachusetts were not registered to vote. Today that figure is at 12.5 percent. Voter turnout is consistent and high among Portuguese-Americans in southern New England. Eighty-three percent (83%) of Portuguese-Americans reported voting in the 1976 election and 80 percent reported voting in the 1996 presidential election. For local elections, the number was 85 percent in 1977 and 81 percent in 2000.

Conclusions and Recommendations

In analyzing the data obtained in the 1977 survey, a rather sophisticated type of statistical analysis was used to determine what factors help us more fully understand and explain the political behavior of the Portuguese residing in a section of New Bedford, Massachusetts and Providence, Rhode Island. The present survey, most importantly, affirms that the explanations and trends identified in that study were on the mark. This fact is extremely important because the body of evidence is now such that it seems to hold over time and to be valid for Portuguese communities residing in different cities. The parallels and contrasts have been defined with substantial confidence so we can now build strategies on something apart from intuitive wisdom and ethnic legend.

The Portuguese behave within their American political world as a group with a very generalized interest in politics, where waves of political information are used to assess a general impact on their condition, and this context creates an active interest in politics resulting in a very narrow focus in behavior–voting. The Portuguese consistently respond to a general involvement with the political. Their behavior can best be characterized as "citizen duty." For the Portuguese, as I stated in 1977, politics is not necessarily something to be understood as a composite of various issue outcomes, but more a general interaction with political institutions that is systemic in nature. They vote and that is how they see their primary responsibility in carrying out the duty of citizenship.

167

In addition, the most important reinforcing mechanism between the system and the citizen for the Portuguese is their assessment of how the system is representing their political interests. If they believe the political system is representing their interests, they support the institution or the person identified with that system. If it is not representing their interest, they walk away from supporting the institution or person. This relation may best explain why Portuguese-Americans so frequently vote for individuals who are not of their own ethnic group. Perhaps the Portuguese, in contrast to other ethnic groups, measure "friendliness to their point of view" on the ethnic band somewhat differently from many other ethnic groups in America. Consequently, in terms of *individual* political behavior, these indices explain the most about how the Portuguese view their political world in the United States. Furthermore, this behavior is not different from the American population at large. In Verba and Nie's landmark 1972 study, the "Voting Specialist"–one of the categories of legitimate participation– was characterized as an individual with low levels of information, low levels of interest in politics, and low levels of political efficacy, but a high frequency of voting as the method of carrying out the duty of citizenship.

As I indicated in 1977, the linkage to cultural determinism in explaining Portuguese political behavior is tenuous at best. History provides a context, but as an explanatory variable it is not particularly salient. The demographic index, which is the one used predominantly in assimilation tests, is also not particularly helpful in explaining individual behavior. Instead, it is my contention that education is the most important variable when viewed within this larger historical and cultural context.

As I have indicated elsewhere, the assimilation of the group, rather than individual assimilation, is probably more important in getting a group to a position of pre-eminence in its political world. Political leadership is needed to effect this assimilation, and generally it is educated candidates—those who speak well, have a public presence, and are articulate—who can explain the issues to the electorate. These types of candidates are more viable because they have to appeal to a constituency wider than just the ethnic group to get elected to public office. In addition, the ethnic group has to achieve some occupational mobility so that it can afford to support its candidates financially in the expensive system of u.s. political campaigns. Furthermore, because the ability to build organizations and networks requires skills and competencies, usually instilled through education, education is important in supporting the structural aspects of political participation and success by an ethnic group. Finally, however, when all is said and done, the Portuguese community needs to pay more attention to political structures in developing a political strategy. The following strategies are appropriate for that reason:

(1) Citizenship and Registration

The Portuguese must continue to support and encourage resident aliens to become u.s. citizens as soon as they are eligible to become citizens. Let us build a positive on the negative of INS pursuits and continue the positive momentum toward increased citizenship among Portuguese-Americans. We also need to focus systematically on voter registration, especially since it appears that the Portuguese vote in very high numbers once they register.

(2) Political Structures in Support of Ethnic Representation

The notion that leaders from the same ethnic group are better representatives of a group's interests is an idea that has a long and deep history in the United States. It has provided the motivating force in local

American politics for more than a century as one wave of immigrants after another has forced its way into mainstream politics. Apparently, the Portuguese have not adopted this view to the same extent as other U.S. ethnic or racial groups. Otherwise, the Portuguese would long ago have captured the mayoralties in Fall River and New Bedford with more consistency and frequency. We know that the type of city charter and smaller electoral units, such as city councils and wards, are institutional structures that seem to produce ethnic candidates more consistent with their numbers in the population. And we also know that in communities where the local party is strong and well-organized the elections result in ethnic majority representation of the type most ethnic groups seek.

169

(3) Building Community

Not only as a Portuguese-American, but as a political scientist and a higher education administrator, my final prescription has to do with a focus on community-building. My parents were members of the Greatest Generation, who survived the Depression and successfully fought the Second World War. And that generation spent a good deal of its time building community. My generation, the Silent Generation, profited greatly from those efforts, which gave rise to the Baby Boomers who protested the injustices and abuses that shocked them from the complacency of the Silents. Generation X, nurtured by affluence and buffered from harms, turned inward and concentrated on individual success with a zeal. Futurists now are predicting that the next generation, the Millennium Generation, has just hit the college campuses. They are more like their great-grandparents than any other generation in that they are committed to developing strategies to make the world a better place, to building community anew, to injecting community life with values of caring and sharing.[14]

I think the Portuguese community should begin to focus on this latest generation. We need to keep them in school, provide them with scholarships so that they can get into college, and we need to support them in athletics so that they can learn to work well in teams. We need to make sure that we afford our young women the same opportunity that we would afford our young men. We need to role-model voluntary activities, and we need to encourage our youth to join the Boy and Girl Scouts of America, the YMCA and YWCA, school groups, the band, and our Portuguese organizations. And we have to encourage them to present themselves for leadership so that they can apprentice and learn the competencies and skills that will allow them to go forth and lead the next generation of Portuguese-Americans. As I concluded in my dissertation many years ago, the Portuguese hold a formidable potential for political power that we must strive together to fulfill.

Notes

[1]This chapter was first delivered as an address at a conference on "Who are the Portuguese?: The New Evidence," sponsored by the Center for Portuguese Studies and Culture, held at the University of Massachusetts Dartmouth, October 28, 2000.

[2]Rita Moniz, "The Portuguese of New Bedford, Massachusetts and Providence, Rhode Island: A Comparative Micro-analysis of Political Attitudes and Behavior," (Ph.D. dissertation, Brown University, 1979).

[3]Rita Duarte Marinho and Elmer E. Cornwell, Os Luso-Americanos No Processo Político Americano: Estudo Duma Situação Concreta (Angra do Heroísmo : Gabinete de Emigração e Apoio às Comunidades Açorianas, 1992).

[4]Sidney Verba and Norman H. Nie, Participation in America (New York: Harper & Row, 1972).

[5]Philip A. Bean, "The Irish, the Italians, and Machine Politics, A Case Study: Utica, NY (1870-1960)," Journal of Urban History 20 (1994): 205-39.

[6]Jerome K. Myers, "Assimilation in the Political Community." Sociology and Social Research 33 (1957):175-82; Reginald Byron, "Ethnicity at the Limit: Ancestry and the Politics of Multiculturalism in the United States," Anthropoligical Journal on European Cultures 8 (1999): 9-30.

[7]The classics of this sociological theory include, Robert A. Dahl, Who Governs? (New Haven: Yale University Press, 1961); Michael, Parenti, "Ethnic Politics and the Persistence of Ethnic Identification," American Political Science Review 61 (1967): 717-26; Edgar Litt, Beyond Pluralism: Ethnic Politics in America. (Glencoe, IL: Scott Foresman, Co., 1970); Raymond E. Wolfinger, The Politics of Progress (New York: Basic Books, 1974); Nathan Glazer and Daniel P. Moynihan, eds.. Ethnicity (Cambridge: Harvard University Press, 1975). For examples that are directly pertinent to Portuguese studies, see, Eleanor Rockwell Edelstein, "From Immigrant to Ethnic: A Study of Portuguese Americans in Bristol, Rhode Island" (Ph.D. dissertation, American University, 1986); Bela Feldman-Bianco, "Multiple Layers of Time and Space: The (Re)Construction of Class, Ethnicity, and Nationalism Among Portuguese Immigrants," [in Portuguese] Revista Crítica de Ciências Sociais 38 (1993): 193-223.

[8]Eugene C. Lee, The Politics of Nonpartisanship: A Study of California City Elections (Berkeley: University of California Press, 1960); Gerald Pomper, "Ethnic and Group Voting in Non-partisan Municipal Elections," Public Opinion Quarterly 30 (1966): 79-97; Willis D. Hawley, Non-partisan Elections and the Case for Party Politics (New York: John Wiley & Sons, 1973); Rita Moniz, "Mayoral Election 1969--New Bedford, Massachusetts: A Case Study," (Brown University. Typescript, 1975); Rita Moniz, "The Politics of Portuguese in America," Portuguese-Times (New Bedford, MA, 1981); Marinho and Elmer E. Cornwell, Os Luso-Americanos No Processo Político Americano: Estudo Duma Situação Concreta.

[9]Doris A. Graber, Mass Media and American Politics (Washington, DC: Congressional Quarterly Press, 1997).

[10]Jeffrey B. Abramson, The Electronic Commonwealth: The Impact of New Media Technologies on Democratic Politics (New York: Basic Books, 1988); Robert M. Entman, Democracy Without Citizens: Media and the Decay of American Politics (New York: Oxford University Press, 1989).

[11]Thomas E. Patterson, The Mass Media Election: How Americans Choose Their President (New York: Praeger, 130).

[12]See Verba and Nie, Participation in America.

[13]Gerald Pomper, "Ethnic and Group Voting in Non-partisan Municipal Elections," pp. 79-97.

[14]See, Chronicle of Higher Education (September 2000).

Methodology and Sample:
Taunton, Massachusetts Survey

Methodology

A "long-form" survey was administered randomly to 104 persons in Census Tract 6137 in Taunton, Massachusetts from October 14, 1999 through May 6, 2000. Fifty-five respondents to the long-form are persons of Portuguese ancestry. The long form was administered to elicit qualitative responses from survey participants about their reasons for participating in political and civic activities. Thus, the long form includes a significant number of open-ended questions designed to elicit spontaneous answers from respondents. The long-form was administered during one-hour interviews in the homes of the respondents. The long-form utilized many questions adapted from the 1972 study by Sidney Verba and Norman H. Nie, *Participation in America.* The interviews also sought to elicit qualitative responses from survey participants about the reasons why they do not participate in political and civic activities. Political scientists routinely conduct studies of voting behavior and civic participation, but there are few studies that explore why people do not participate in politics and civil society.[1]

A bilingual survey assistant was employed to conduct the key informant interviews with the long-form in Census Tract 6137. The survey assistant was trained in survey techniques by staff at the Center for Policy Analysis. The surveys were conducted during daylight hours, with households to be interviewed selected on a random basis in the field.

A "short-form" telephone survey was administered to a random sample of 300 additional respondents in the same census tract from April 15, 2000 to May 13, 2000. The short form survey was administered to generate comparative data concerning the levels and types of political and civic participation among Portuguese and non-Portuguese residents of Taunton. The short-form survey is designed only to solicit quantitative comparisons about the levels and types of participation.

All questions on the short-form survey were included in the long-form survey, although the long form included additional questions to explore in greater detail the reasons for participation and non-participation among Portuguese-Americans. The results of both surveys are statistically similar on the common questions, so there is a high level of confidence that the long form data and open-ended responses are a reliable and valid representation of activity and opinion among Portuguese-Americans in Taunton, Massachusetts. The long- and short-form surveys combined generated valid responses from one adult in 23.6 percent of the 1,710 households in Census Tract 6137.

In cases where questions from the two survey forms are identical, the results have been merged,[2] while the results of those questions unique to the long-form survey are discussed separately. Where appropriate, a Pearson chi-square test of independence was conducted to identify variables that reveal a statistically significant correlation with political and civic participation, although far more sophisticated statistical techniques would be required to advance causal statements.[3]

Furthermore, the small size of the sub-samples for other ethnic groups, such as African-Americans, Hispanics, and Asian-Americans does not permit comparison between Portuguese-Americans and other distinct ethnic or racial groups. Hence, given the small size of the African-American, Hispanic, and Asian-American populations in Southeastern Massachusetts, the comparisons between Portuguese and "non-Portuguese" respondents are largely comparisons among persons of different ancestry within the census category of White Caucasian. Similarly, while the size of the Portuguese sub-sample is sufficient for making some tentative observations about differences within the Portuguese community—for example, between United States born and foreign-born Portuguese-Americans – these findings should be taken only as a guide for future inquiry, rather than as a basis for bold generalizations.

Sample

Educational Attainment
More than three-quarters (78.0%) of the survey respondents report that they have at least a high school diploma (see Table 1), while 23.5

percent report having a bachelor's degree or higher. There is a significant relationship between respondents' ethnicity and educational attainment. For example, the average last grade completed by non-Portuguese respondents is 13.8 years compared to 10.6 years for Portuguese respondents. Only 6.6 percent of non-Portuguese respondents report not having a high school diploma, while 45.5 percent of Portuguese respondents report not having a high school diploma. Similarly, nearly two-thirds (65.5%) of non-Portuguese respondents report having some college education – either an associate's degree, a bachelor's degree, or higher – while only about one quarter (24.6%) of Portuguese respondents report the same.

173

TABLE 1

EDUCATIONAL ATTAINMENT

Attainment	All Respondents Number/Percent		Portuguese Percent	Non-Portuguese Percent
No Diploma	74	22.0%	45.5%	6.6%
At least a Diploma	97	28.9%	29.9%	27.9%
Some College Associate's	86	25.6%	11.9%	35.5%
Bachelor's or Higher	79	23.5%	12.7%	30.0%

Family Income
The median family income of survey respondents is between $35,000 and $45,000, which is consistent with slow-to-stagnant income growth in Southeastern Massachusetts during the last ten years (see Table 2).[4] In general, Portuguese respondents have lower family incomes than non-Portuguese respondents and these differences are statistically significant.

Age
The median age of the respondents is 45.0 years. The average of Portuguese respondents (49.0) was somewhat higher than the average age of non-Portuguese respondents (41.0) (see Table 3).

Sex
Fifty-five percent (55.0%) of the survey respondents are female and 45.0 percent (45.0%) are male (see Table 4).

TABLE 2

Annual Family Income	All Respondents Number/Percent		Portuguese Percent	Non-Portuguese Percent
less than $15,000	43	12.8%	19.7%	8.1%
$15,000 to $25,000	34	10.1%	16.1%	6.1%
$25,000 to $35,000	43	13.1%	13.9%	12.2%
$35,000 to $45,000	68	20.2%	13.9%	24.9%
$45,000 to $60,000	62	18.4%	17.5%	19.3%
$60,000 to $150,000	79	24.0%	19.0%	26.9%
$150,000 or more	5	1.5%	0.0%	2.5%

174

TABLE 3

Age Group	All Respondents Number/Percent	
18 to 25	58	14.6%
26 to 35	75	18.8%
36 to 45	69	17.3%
46 to 55	83	20.9%
56 to 65	44	11.1%
65 and over	69	17.3%

TABLE 4

Sex	All Respondents Number/Percent		Portuguese Percent	Non-Portuguese Percent
Female	220	55.0$	52.6$	56.9$
Male	180	45.0$	47.4$	43.1$

TABLE 5

Race/Ethnicity	All Respondents Number/Percent	
African American	5	1.2%
American Indian	2	0.5%
Cape Verdean	10	2.5%
Hispanic	3	0.7%
Other	4	1.0%
Portuguese	153	38.2%
White Caucasian	224	55.9%

Race and Ethnicity

The residents of Census Tract 6137 are overwhelmingly white Caucasian (96.7%) with a sprinkling of African-American (1.1%) and Hispanic (1.9%) residents. The sample accurately reflects this mix based on the 1990 Census (see Table 5).

[1]Herbert Hirsch, *Poverty and Politicization: Political Socialization in an American Sub-culture* (New York: Free Press, 1971).

[2]There is a 4.9 percent margin of error on the merged survey at a confidence interval of 95 percent. This means that if a question from the survey was asked 100 times, 95 of those times the percentage of people giving a particular answer to the question would be within 4.9 points of the percentage who gave the same answer in this poll.

[3]For this study, variables are considered statistically significant if the Pearson chi-square is .05 and below. While the Pearson chi-square value determines the correlation between two variables, one can not assume from this number that one variable causes the other; correlation is merely a measure of the extent to which different variables change together. Correlation analysis alone does not allow the researcher to control for other relevant variables and it does not determine causality between variables. However, the purpose of this report is to offer a descriptive analysis of the findings and more advanced techniques may be used in the future.

[4]Clyde W. Barrow, "Southeastern Massachusetts: A Region of Growth Without Development," *Massachusetts Benchmarks,* Vol. 1, No. 3 (Summer 1998): 9-10, 15-17.

[5]At the time of publication, the 2000 data for ancestry, educational attainment, and income had not been released by the U.S. Census Bureau and it was not scheduled to be released for several months.

APPENDIX B

METHODOLOGY: POLITICAL EFFICACY, ECONOMIC VIEWS, AND CULTURAL ISSUES

Geography

The political efficacy (Chapter 3), economic views (Chapter 4), and social and cultural issues (Chapter 5) surveys were administered to adult (age 18+) residents of households living in the "Portuguese Archipelago" of Southeastern Massachusetts. Southeastern Massachusetts consists of 48 cities and towns in Bristol, Plymouth, and Norfolk Counties. The region is 1,224 square miles in area and has a population of 949,520 (U.S. Census 1990). The major cities in the region, which account for about 39 percent of the region's population, are Attleboro, Brockton, Fall River, New Bedford, and Taunton. The Portuguese Archipelago of Southeastern Massachusetts includes eighteen cities and towns in Bristol and Plymouth Counties. The three major cities in the Portuguese Archipelago – Fall River, New Bedford, and Taunton -- account for more than half of the area's population (58.3%). The Portuguese Archipelago is 511 square miles in area and has a population of 415,896 (1990) (Chapter 1, Figure 1).

Telephone Interviews
The Center for Policy Analysis uses the Genesys Sampling System to generate random telephone numbers for all telephone surveys. The Genesys Sampling System is used by many major survey organizations, including university research centers, private marketing consultants, and public opinion polling firms. The system uses a list of all possible telephone numbers in the United States and then randomly generates a telephone sample for a designated geographic area. The sample is generated using random digit dialing (RDD), which insures an equal and known probability of selection for every residential telephone number in the polling area. To facilitate efficiency in polling, the original list of possible numbers is "cleaned" so far as possible of disconnected numbers, cellular telephone numbers, facsimile machines, and

places of business. This sampling procedure was used in the surveys of political efficacy, economic opinions, and opinions on social and cultural issues.

However, the RDD sampling method is not reliable for a small geographic area such as a census tract, since a large percentage of telephone numbers with the same three-digit prefix normally fall outside the census tract area. Consequently, the Taunton survey was conducted using a "listed sample" derived from the White Pages listings for Census Tract 6137. The listed sample does have drawbacks, such as excluding households who recently moved to the neighborhood and households with an unlisted telephone number.

The telephone interviews were conducted between 9:00 am and 9:00 pm on weekdays and between 11:00 am and 3:00 pm on Saturdays. This range of hours provides the interviewers an opportunity to contact hard-to-reach respondents. All "no answer" telephone numbers were called at least seven times at varying times of the day, including weekends, before they were considered unreachable. The Center's senior staff constantly monitored the progress of interview outcomes and each block of telephone numbers to prevent problem cases that could interfere with the integrity of the survey procedures. The survey procedures used by the Center for Policy Analysis adhere to the highest quality academic and government research standards.

A total of 401 telephone interviews were conducted for the political efficacy survey from June 1, 2000 to July 14, 2000 with a margin of error +/- 5 percent. A total of 400 telephone interviews were conducted for the economic opinions survey from April 15, 2000 to May 13, 2000 with a margin of error of +/- 5 percent. A total of 400 telephone interviews were conducted for the social and cultural issues survey from August 7, 2000 to October 11, 2000 with a margin of error +/- 5 percent.

Tests of Significance
A Pearson chi-square test of independence was conducted to determine which variables reveal a statistically significant correlation with each other. The Pearson Chi-square is the most common test for significance of the relationship between categorical variables. This statistic is used to test the measure of association between columns and rows in

tabular data. It tests the hypothesis of no association of columns and rows in tabular data. For this study, the correlation between variables is considered statistically significant if the Pearson chi-square and the Pearson Correlation coefficient is .05 and below. While the Pearson chi-square value determines the correlation between two variables, correlation analysis alone does not allow the researcher to determine causality between variables. Also, in some cases, two variables that move together may be driven simultaneously by a third variable. In cases such as these, partial correlations were run to control for, or partial out, the effects of a third factor thought to drive the relationship between the two variables of interest.

BIBLIOGRAPHY:

Ethnic Politics and Portuguese-American Political Participation
*Nancy Lambert, Rita Duarte Marinho, and Clyde W. Barrow**

Abramson, Jeffrey B. 1988. *The Electronic Commonwealth: The Impact of New Media Technologies on Democratic Politics.* New York: Basic Books.

Aguirre, B. E., Rogelio Saenz, and Sean-Shong Hwang. 1989. "Discrimination and the Assimilation and Ethnic Competition Perspectives." *Social Science Quarterly* 70:594-606.

Aho, William. 1967. "Differences in Occupational and Educational Attainments of Second Generation American Males of United Kingdom, German, and Italian Parentage." *Research Reports in the Social Sciences* 1:50-60.

Alba, Richard D., John R. Logan, and Kyle Crowder. 1997. "White Ethnic Neighborhoods and Assimilation: The Greater New York Region, 1980-1990." *Social Forces* 75:883-912.

Al-Khajardzi, Majid G., and M. Emilie. 1970. *Immigration and Beyond: The Portuguese Community of New Bedford, Massachusetts.* New Bedford, Massachusetts: Onboard of New Bedford.

Allen, Everett S. 1973. *Children of the Light: The Rise and Fall of New Bedford Whaling and the Death of the Artic Fleet.* Boston: Little, Brown, and Co.

Allswang, John M. 1971. *A House for All Peoples.* Kentucky: University of Kentucky Press.

Almond, Gabriel, and Sidney Verba. 1963. *The Civic Culture.* Princeton: Princeton University Press.

Almond, Gabriel and Sidney Verba. 1980. *The Civic Culture Revisited: An Analytic Study.* Boston: Little Brown.

179

Andrade, Steven, Clyde W. Barrow, and David R. Borges. 2001. *Strategies for Recruiting, Retaining and Training the Workforce of Tomorrow: A Blueprint for Action.* Boston: Donahue Institute and Greater Bristol Workforce Investment Board.

Araujo, Sarita A. 1996. "Portuguese Families." In Monica McGoldrick and Joe Giordano, eds. *Ethnicity and Family Therapy,* 2nd ed. New York: Guilford Press.

Baganha, Maria Ioannis Benis. 1991. "The Social Mobility of Portuguese Immigrants in the United States at the Turn of the Nineteenth Century." *International Migration Review* 25:277-302.

Bailey, Harry A., and Ellis Katz. 1969. *Ethnic Group Politics.* Columbus, OH: Merrill and Co.

Banfield, Edward C., and James Q. Wilson. 1963. *City Politics.* Cambridge: Harvard University Press.

Banfield, Edward C., and James Q. Wilson. 1963. *Political Influence.* New York: The Free Press.

Baptista, Frank B. 2001. "Voz do Emigrante: Politics Focus of Study." *The Fall River Sunday Herald News,* January 7, pp. B1-B2.

Baptista, Frank B. 2001. "Voz do Emigrante: Study Shows Range of Views." *The Fall River Sunday Herald News,* January 14, pp. B1-B2.

Baptista, Frank B. 2001. "Voz do Emigrante." *The Fall River Sunday Herald News,* January 21, pp. B1-B2.

Barmann, Timothy C. 1998. "Portuguese Newspaper's Fate Is in Doubt: *O Jornal,* One of Two Portuguese-Language Newspapers in the Region, Will Soon Be Shut Down If its Parent Company Cannot Find a Buyer." *Providence Journal Bulletin* 2 August, sec. 7, p. A-1.

Barrow, Clyde W. 1998. "Southeastern Massachusetts: A Region of Growth Without Development." *Massachusetts Benchmarks,* Vol. 1, No. 3 (Summer 1998):9-10, 15-17.

Barrow, Clyde W. and David R. Borges. 2001. *Greater New Bedford Economic Base Analysis.* North Dartmouth, MA: Center for Policy Analysis and Greater New Bedford Workforce Investment Board.

Bean, Philip A. 1994. "The Irish, the Italians, and Machine Politics, A Case Study: Utica, NY (1870-1960)." *Journal of Urban History* 20:205-39.

Becker, Adeline. 1990. "The Role of the School in the Maintenance and Change of Ethnic Group Affiliation." *Human Organization* 49:48-55.

Bell, Daniel. 1976. *The Coming of the Postindustrial Society: A Venture in Social Forecasting.* New York: Basic Books.

Bellias, G. A. 1970. *The American Revolution: How Revolutionary Was It?* New York: Holt, Rinehard & Wilson.

Bennett, Marion T. 1963. *American Immigration Politics: A History.* Washington, DC: Public Affairs Press.

Bernard, William S. 1967. "The Integration of Immigrants in the United States." *International Migration Review* 1:23-32.

Blalock, Hubert M., Jr., and Ann B. Blalock. 1968. *Methodology in Social Research.* New York: McGraw-Hill.

Bluestone, Barry. 1982. *The Deindustrialization of America: Plant Closings, Community Abandonment, and the Dismantling of Basic Industries.* New York: Basic Books.

Bogardus, Emory S. 1930. "Mexican Immigrants and Segregation." *American Journal of Sociology* 36:74-80.

Borges, David R. and Clyde W. Barrow. 2001. *Fall River Community Report Card* 2000. North Dartmouth, MA : Center for Policy Analysis.

Bossard, James S. 1945. "The Bilingual as a Person–Linguistic Identification with Status." *American Sociological Review,* Vol. 10, No.6 (December):699-709

Boutte, Marie I. 1992. "Festas Do Espirito Santo: Portuguese Celebrations in Nevada." *Halcyon* 14:231-46.

Breton, Raymond, and Maurice Pinard. 1960. "Group Formation Among Immigrants: Criteria and Processes." *Canadian Journal of Economics and Political Science* 25:465-77.

Breton, Raymond. 1964. "Institutional Completeness of Ethnic Communities and the Personal Relations of Immigrants." *American Journal of Sociology* 70:193-205.

Brocly, E. B. 1969. "Migration and Adaptation: The Nature of the Problem." *American Behavioral Scientist* 13:5-13.

Brod, Richard and Bettina J. Huber. 1997. "Foreign Language Enrollments in United States Institutions of Higher Education, Fall 1995." *ADFL Bulletin*, Vol. 28, No. 2 (Winter):1-7.

Byron, Reginald. 1999. "Ethnicity at the Limit. Ancestry and the Politics of Multiculturalism in the United States." *Anthropoligical Journal on European Cultures* 8:9-30.

Cabral, Stephen L. 1989. *Tradition and Transformation: Portuguese Feasting in New Bedford.* New York: AMS Press, Inc.

Campbell, Angus, Philip E. Converse, Warren E. Miller, and Donald E. Stokes. 1960. *The American Voter.* New York: John Wiley & Sons, Inc.

Campbell, Bruce J. 1954. *The Golden Door: The Irony of Our Immigration Policy.* New York: Random House.

Campbell, Donald T., and Julian C., Stanley. 1963. *Experimental and Quasi-Experimental Designs for Research.* Chicago: Rand McNally.

Campisi, Paul. 1947. "A Scale for the Measurement of Acculturation." Ph.D. dissertation., University of Chicago.

Campisi, Paul. 1948. "Ethnic Family Patterns: The Italian Family in the U.S." *American Journal of Sociology* 53:443-49.

Carey, Peter and G. Carter Bentley, eds. 1995. *East Timor at the Crossroads: The Forgin of a Nation*. Honolulu: University of Hawaii Press.

Cecci, Camillo. 1967. "Ethnic Identification in Second and Third Generation Emigrants." *Studi Emigrazione* 4:209-52.

Center on Policy Attitudes. 1999. "Expecting More Say" in *The American Public on Its Role in Government Decision Making*. Washington, DC.

Chapa, Jorge. 1995. "Mexican-American Class Structure and Political Participation." *New England Journal of Public Policy*, Vol. 2, No. 1 (Spring/Summer):183-98.

Chen, Kevin. 1992. *Political Alienation and Voting Turnout in the United States, 1960-1988*. San Francisco: Mellon Research University Press.

"Civic League Plans Citizenship Drive." 1936. *The Providence Journal*, May 16, p. 9.

Cobb, Roger W., and Charles D. Elder. 1972. *Participation in American Politics: The Dynamics of Agenda-Building*. Baltimore: Johns Hopkins Press.

Cochran, David Carroll. 1995/96. "Ethnic Diversity and Democratic Stability: The Case of Irish Americans." *Political Science Quarterly*, 10:587-604.

Cochran, William G. 1963. *Sampling Techniques*, 2nd ed. New York: John Wiley & Sons, Inc.

Commission on the Skills of the American Workforce. 1990. *America's Choice: High Skills or Low Wages!* Rochester, NY: National Center on Education and the Economy.

Commons, John R. 1967. *Races and Immigrants in America*. New York: Augustus M. Kelley Publishers.

Cordasco, Francesco. 1975. "Spanish Speaking Children in American Schools." *International Migration Review* 9:379-82.

Cornwell, Elmer E., Jr. 1960. "Party Absorption of Ethnic Groups: The Case of Providence, Rhode Island." *Social Forces* 38:205-10.

Crenson, Matthew. 1971. *The Unpolitics of Air Pollution.* Baltimore: Johns Hopkins Press.

Crosby, Katherine K. 1925. "Boston Portuguese Work Hard in Drab Environment." *Boston Herald,* January 25, p. 6.

Cruz, Jose. 1995. "Puerto Rican Politics in the United States: A Preliminary Assessment." *New England Journal of Public Policy,* Vol. 2, No. 1 (Spring/Summer):199-219.

Cruz, Jose E. 1996. "Puerto Ricans and Politics in the United States: A Preliminary Evaluation." *Revista de Ciencias Sociales* 1:86-111.

"Cultural Assimilation of Immigrants." 1950. UNESCO Supplement to *Population Studies,* March.

Curriculum Research and Development Center. 1997. *The Need to Develop a System for the Assessment/Testing of Portuguese Speaking Students.* Kingston, RI: University of Rhode Island.

Dahl, Robert A. 1961. *Who Governs?* New Haven: Yale University Press.

Dahl, Robert A. 1971. *Polyarchy: Participation and Opposition* New Haven: Yale University Press.

Dawson, Richard E., and Kenneth Prewitt. 1969. *Political Socialization.* Boston: Little, Brown and Co.

DeConde, Alexander, Armin Rappaport and William Steckel. 1968. *Patterns in American History,* Vol. 2. California: Wadsworth Publishing Co., Inc.

Deming, William Edwards. 1950. *Some Theory of Sampling.* New York: John Wiley & Sons, Inc.

Derthick, Martha. 1972. *New Towns, In-Town.* Washington, DC: The Urban Institute.

Dinnerstein, Leonard, and David M. Reimers. 1999. *Ethnic Americans: A History of Immigration,* 4th ed. New York: Columbia University Press.

Dion, Marc Munroe. 2000. "Seminar Explores Portuguese Issues." *The Herald News,* October 29, p. B2.

Divine, Robert A. 1957. *American Immigration Policy: 1924-1952.* New Haven: Yale University Press.

Dolbeare, Kenneth M., and Linda J. Medcalf. 1993. *American Ideologies: Shaping the New Politics of the 1990s,* 2nd ed. New York: McGraw-Hill, Inc.

Edelstein, Eleanor Rockwell. 1986. "From Immigrant to Ethnic: A Study of Portuguese Americans in Bristol, Rhode Island." Ph.D. dissertation, American University.

Eisenstadt, S. N. 1951. "The Place of Elites and Primary Groups in the Absorption of New Immigrants in Israel." *American Journal of Sociology* 57:222-31.

Eisenstadt, S. N. 1953. "Analysis of Patterns of Immigration and Absorption of Immigrants." *Population Studies* 7:167-80.

Eisenstadt, S. N. 1955. *The Absorption of Immigrants: A Comparative Study Based on the Jewish Community of Palestine and the State of Israel.* Glencoe, IL: The Free Press.

Entman, Robert M. 1989. *Democracy Without Citizens: Media and the Decay of American Politics.* New York: Oxford University Press.

Erie, Steven. 1990. *Rainbow's End: Irish Americans and the Dilemmas of Urban Machine Politics.* Berkeley and Los Angeles: University of California Press.

Erikson, Robert S., Norman R. Luttberg, and Kent L. Tedin. 1991. *American Public Opinion,* 4th ed. New York: Macmillan Co.

Feldman-Bianco, Bela. 1993. "Multiple Layers of Time and Space: The (Re)Construction of Class, Ethnicity, and Nationalism Among Portuguese Immigrants." *Revista Crítica de Ciências Socias* 38:193-223.

Fenton, John H. 1960. *The Catholic Vote.* New Orleans: Hauser Press.

Ferreira, João. 2000. "Portuguese-Americans Wield Untapped Power, Study Says." *New Bedford Sunday Standard-Times,* October 22, pp. C1-C2.

Ferreira, João. 2000. "Portuguese Primed for Progress." *New Bedford Sunday Standard-Times,* October 29, pp. A1, A4.

Festinger, Leon, and Daniel Katz. 1966. *Research Methods in the Behavioral Sciences.* New York: Holt, Rinehart and Wilson.

Fishman, Joshua, and Vladimir C. Nahirny. 1964. "The Ethnic Group School and Mother Tongue Maintenance in the United States." *Sociology of Education* 37:306-17.

Fishman, Joshua, et al.. 1966. *Language Loyalty in the United States: The Maintenance and Perpetuation of Non-English Mother Tongues by American Ethnic and Religious Groups.* Mouton: The Hague.

Fitzpatrick, Joseph P. 1966. "The Importance of Community in the Process of Immigrant Assimilation." *International Migration Review* 1:5-15.

Forcese, Dennis P., and Stephen Richer, eds. 1970. *Stages of Social Research: Contemporary Perspectives.* Englewood Cliffs, NJ: Prentice-Hall.

Frances, E. K. 1912. "Variables in the Formation of So-called Minority Groups." *American Journal of Sociology* 6:6-14.

Frohlich, Norman, Joe A. Oppenheimer, and Oran A. Young. 1971. *Political Leadership and Collective Goods.* Princeton, New Jersey: Princeton University Press.

Fuchs, Lawrence H. 1956. *Political Behavior of American Jews.* Glencoe, IL: The Free Press.

Fuchs, Lawrence. 1991. *The American Kaleidoscope: Ethnicity and the Civic Culture.*Hanover, NH: University Press of New England.

Fugita, Stephen S., and David J. O'Brien. 1985. "Structural Assimilation, Ethnic Group Membership, and Political Participation among Japanese Americans: A Research Note." *Social Forces* 63:986-95.

Gabriel, Richard A. 1963. *The Ethnic Factor in the Urban Polity.* New York: MSS Information Corporation.

Gallup. 2000. www.gallup.com/poll/soc_issues.asp

Gans, Herbert J. 1999. "Filling in Some Holes: Six Areas of Needed Immigration Research." *American Behavioral Scientist* 42:1302-13.

Gans, Herbert. 1962. *The Urban Villagers.* New York: The Free Press, 1962.

Garcia, John A. 1987. "The Political Integration of Mexican Immigrants: Examining Some Political Orientations." *International Migration Review* 21:372-89.

Geczy, Zoltan. 1988. "Revolution and Identity: The Influence of Political Events on the Process of Assimilation." Ph.D. dissertation, Fordham University.

Gerstle, Gary. 2001. *The American Crucible: Race and Nation in the Twentieth Century.* Princeton: Princeton University Press.

Geschwender, James A., Rita Carroll-Seguin, and Howard Brill. 1988. "The Portuguese and Haoles of Hawaii: Implications for the Origin of Ethnicity." *American Sociological Review* 53:515-27.

Gilbert, Dorothy A. 1989. *Recent Portuguese Immigrants to Fall River, Massachusetts: An Analysis of Relative Economic Success.* New York : AMS Press, Inc.

187

Gilmore, Robert S. and Robert B. Lamb. 1975. *Political Alienation in Contemporary America.* New York: St. Martin's Press.

Glazer, Nathan and Daniel P. Moynihan, eds. 1975. *Ethnicity.* Cambridge: Harvard University Press.

Glazer, Nathan, and Daniel P. Moynihan, eds. 1970. *Beyond the Melting Pot,* 2nd ed. Cambridge: MIT Press.

"Go West, Portuguese: They Did, Says Book." 2000. *The Providence Journal-Bulletin,* August 3, p. B-7.

Gobetz, Giles Edward. 1966. "The Ethnic Ethics of Assimilation: Slovenian View." *Phylon 27* (Fall):268-73.

Goldstein, Sidney. 1968. *Jewish Americans: Three Generations in a Jewish Community.* Englewood Cliffs, NJ: Prentice-Hall.

Gonzalez, Juan. 2001. *Harvest of Empire: A History of Latinos in America.* New York: Penguin.

Gordon, Daniel N. 1970. "Immigrants and Municipal Voting Turnout: Implications for the Changing Ethnic Impact on Voter Turnout." *American Sociological Review* 35:665-81.

Gordon, Milton. 1964. *Assimilation in American Life.* New York: Oxford University Press.

Gottfried, Alex. 1962. *Boss Cermak of Chicago.* Seattle: University of Washington Press.

Graber, Doris A. 1997. *Mass Media and American Politics.* Washington, DC: Congressional Quarterly Press.

Grebler, Leo. 1966 "The Naturalization of Mexican Immigrants in the United States." *International Migration Review* 1(1):17-31.

Greeley, Andrew M., and William C. McCready. 1971. *Why Can't They Be Like Us?* New York: Dutton Press.

Greeley, Andrew M., and William C. McCready. 1974. *Ethnicity in the United States: A Preliminary Reconnaissance.* New York: John Wiley & Sons.

Greenstone, David, and Paul Peterson. 1973. *Race and Authority in Urban Politics.* New York: Russell Sage Foundation.

Grossman, Elliot. 2000. "Pride in Portugal: The Language and the Homeland Keep Portuguese, Immigrants in the Lehigh Valley Connected to Their Country." (Series: Census 2000 Focus on Community: Last in an Occasional Series) *Allentown Morning Call* (Pennsylvania), November 1.

Hackett, Walter. 1968. "Portuguese Navigate Mainstream, U.S.A." *Providence Sunday Journal,* December 4, p. 34.

Hainsworth, Paul and Stephen McCloskey, eds. 2000. *The East Timor Question: The Struggle for Independence from Indonesia.* New York: I.B. Tauris.

Hall, Prescott F. 1907. *Immigration and Its Effects Upon the United States.* New York: Henry Holt & Co.

Hall-Arber, Madeleine. 1996. "Hear Me Speak: Italian and Portuguese Women Facing Fisheries Management." *Anthropoligica* 38:221-48.

Handlin, Oscar. 1959. *Immigration as a Factor in American History.* Englewood Cliffs, NJ: Prentice-Hall, Inc.

Handlin, Oscar. 1973. *The Uprooted.* Boston: Little, Brown & Co.

Hansen, Marcus L. 1940. *The Immigrant in American History.* New York: Harper & Row Publishers.

Hansen, Morris H., et al. 1953. *Sample Survey Methods and Theory,* Vol. II. New York: John Wiley & Sons.

Hawkins, Brett W., and Robert A. Larinskas. 1970. *Ethnic Factor in American Politics.* Columbus, OH: Charles E. Merrill Publishing Co.

Hawley, Willis D. 1973. *Non-partisan Elections and the Case for Party Politics.* New York: John Wiley & Sons.

Heer, David M. 1961. "The Marital Status of Second Generation Americans." *American Review* (April):233-39.

Heiss, Jerold. 1966. "Sources of Satisfaction and Assimilation Among Italian Immigrants." *Human Relations* 14:165-77.

Heiss, Jerold. 1967. "Factors Related to Immigrant Assimilation: The Early Post-Migration Situation." *Human Organization* 26:265-72.

Hess, Robert D., and Judith V. Torney. 1967. *The Development of Political Attitudes in Children.* Garden City, New York: Doubleday and Co.

Higham, John. 1963. *Strangers in the Land.* New York: Atheneum.

Hine, Lewis. 1984. "Lewis Hine on the Cranberry Bogs." *Spinner: People and Culture in Southeastern Massachusetts.*" 3:66-9.

Hirsch, Herbert. 1971. *Poverty and Politicization: Political Socialization in an American Sub-culture.* New York: Free Press.

Hirschman, Philip Kasinitz, and Josh DeWind eds. 1999. *The Handbook of International Migration: The American Experience.* New York: Russell Sage.

Hoffmann, Stanley. 1968. *Gulliver's Troubles, or the Setting of American Foreign Policy.* New York: McGraw-Hill Book Co.

Hofstadter, Richard. 1955. *The Age of Reform.* New York: Alfred A. Knopf, Inc.

Hofstadter, Richard. 1963. *The Progressive Movement 1900-1915.* Englewood Cliffs, NJ: Prentice-Hall, Inc.

Hollingshead, August B. 1950. "Cultural Factors in the Selection of Marriage Mates." *American Sociological Review* 15:619-27.

Hopkins, Lorraine L. 1967. "The New Immigrants." *Providence Sunday Journal,* September 17, pp. 18-22.

Horowitz, Irving Louis, and Martin Liebowitz. 1968. "Social Deviance and Political Marginality: Toward a Redefinition of the Relation Between Sociology and Politics." *Social Problems* 15 (Winter):280-96.

Howitt, Arnold M. 1976. "Strategies of Governing: Electoral Constraints on Mayoral Behavior in Philadelphia and Boston." Ph.D. dissertation, Harvard University.

Howitt, Arnold M., and Rita Moniz. 1976. "Ethnic Identity, Political Organization, and Political Structure." Presented at the annual meeting of American Political Science Association.

Hudson, Robert, and Fred Reno. eds. 2000. *Politics of Identity: Migrants and Minorities in Multicultural States.* London: Macmillan.

Huff, Toby E. 1989. "Education and Ethnicity in Southeastern Massachusetts." *New England Board of Higher Education: Issues in Planning and Policymaking.* (December) 1-8.

Hutchinson, E. P. 1956. *Immigrants and Their Children: 1850–1950.* New York: John Wiley and Sons.

Ianni, Francis A. J. 1957. "Residential and Occupational Mobility as Indices of the Acculturation of an Ethnic Group." *Social Forces* 36:65-72.

Ianni, Francis A. J. 1961. "The Italo-American Teenager." *Annals of the American Academy of Political and Social Science* 338:70-78.

Immigrants Assistance Center. 1977. *Annual Report.* New Bedford, MA.

"Inquerito do Centro de Estudos Portugueses da UMass Dartmouth Revela."2000. *Portuguese Times,* November 9, p.1.

Jennings, M. Kent, and Richard G. Niemi. 1968. "The Transmission of Political Values from Parent to Child." *American Political Science Review* 62:169-84.

Johnson, Albert R. 1938. "30,489 Portuguese-Americans in Rhode Island Depend on Consul in Many Problems." *The Providence Journal,* January 31.

Johnston, William B. 1987. *Workforce 2000: Work and Workers for the Twenty-First Century.* Indianapolis: Hudson Institute.

Jones, Frank E. 1956. "A Sociological Perspective on Immigrant Adjustment." *Social Forces* 35:39-47.

Jovanovic, Goran. 1995. "From Immigrants to Ethnic Minorities: Southern Italians, Eastern European Jews and Poles in America, 1880-1924." *Socioloski Pregled* 29:59-76.

Jun, Sung Pyo, and Gordon M. Armstrong. 1997. "Status Inconsistency and Striving for Power in a Church: Is Church a Refuge or a Stepping-Stone?" *Korea Journal of Population and Development* 26(1):103-129.

Jung, Moon-Kie. 1999. "No Whites, No Asians: Race, Marxism, and Hawaii's Preemergent Working Class." *Social Science History* 23:357-93.

Junn, Jane. 1999. "Participation in Liberal Democracy: The Political Assimilation of Immigrants and Ethnic Minorities in the United States." *American Behavioral Scientist* 2:1417-38.

Kantowicz, Edward R. 1975. *Polish-American Politics in Chicago 1888-1940.* Chicago: University of Chicago Press.

Karpathakis, Anna. 1999. "Home Society Politics and Immigrant Political Incorporation: The Case of Greek Immigrants in New York City." *International Migration Review* 33: 55-78.

Katz, Ellis. 1969. *Ethnic Group Politics.* Columbus, OH: Merrill and Co.

Katznelson, Ira. 1973. *Black Men, White Cities.* New York: Oxford University Press.

Kimball, Penn. 1972. *The Disconnected.* New York: Columbia University Press.

King, Alan J. C. 1968. "Ethnicity and School Adjustment." *Canadian Review of Sociology and Anthropology* 5:84-91.

Kjolseth, Roif. 1970. "Bilingual Education Programs in the United States: For Assimilation or Pluralism." Presented at the Event World Congress of Sociology, Varna, Bulgaria.

Kluckhorn, Florence. 1958. "Family Diagnosis: Variations in the Basic Values of Family Systems." *Social Casework* 39:63-73.

Kohler, Max J. 1936. *Immigrants and Aliens in the United States.* New York: Bloch Publishing Co.

Kroehler, Al L., and Talcott Parsons. 1958. "The Concepts of Culture and Social System." *American Sociological Review* 23:582-3.

Lacroix, Max, and Edith Adams. 1950. "Statistics for Studying the Cultural Assimilation of Immigrants." Special Supplement to *Population Studies* (March):69-97.

Ladd, Everett Carl. 1975. *Transformations of the American Party System: Political Coalitions from the New Deal to the 1970s.* New York: W.W. Norton and Co.,Inc.

Ladd, Everett Carl. 1978. *Where Have All the Voters Gone? The Fracturing of America's Political Parties.* New York: W.W. Norton and Co.,Inc.

Lanca, Margaret, Christine Alksnis, Neil J. Roese, and Robert C. Gardner. 1994. "Effects of Language Choice on Acculturation: A Study of Portuguese Immigrants in a Multicultural Setting." *Journal of Language and Social Psychology* 13(3):315-30.

Lane, Robert. 1959. *Political Life.* New York: The Free Press.

Lee, Eugene C. 1960. *The Politics of Nonpartisanship: A Study of California City Elections.* Berkeley: University of California Press.

Levy, Clifford J. 1995. "A Portuguese Village in Newark." *New York Times,* October 6, sec. C, p. 1.

Levy, Mark R., and Michael S. Kramer. 1972. *The Ethnic Factor: How America's Minorities Decide Elections.* New York: Simon & Schuster.

Lewin, Kurt. 1948. *Social Conflict.* New York: Harper and Brothers.

Lewis, Edward R. 1928. *America: Nation or Confusion.* New York: Harper and Brothers.

193

Lick, Sue F. 1998. *Stories Grandma Never Told: Portuguese Women in California*. Berkeley, CA: Heyday Books.

Lieberson, Stanley. 1963. "The Old-New Distinction and Immigrants in Australia." *American Sociological Review* 28:550-64.

Lieberson, Stanley. 1963. *Ethnic Patterns in American Cities*. Glencoe, IL: The Free Press.

Lindzey, Gardner, and Elliot Aronson, eds. 1969. *The Handbook of Social Psychology*, Volumes III-IV. Reading, MA: Adison-Wesley Publishing, Co.

Lineberry, Robert L., and Ira Sharkansky. 1971. *Urban Politics and Public Policy*. New York: Harper & Row.

Lipsky, Michael. 1968. "Protest as a Political Resource." *American Political Science Review* 62:1146.

Litt, Edgar. 1963. "Civic Education, Community Norms and Social Indoctrination." *American Sociological Review* 28:69-75.

Litt, Edgar. 1970. *Ethnic Politics in America: Beyond Pluralism*. Glenview, IL: Scott Foresman and Co.

Lopata, Helen Z. 1976. *Status Competition in an Ethnic Community*. Englewood Cliffs, NJ: Prentice-Hall.

Lorinskas, Robert A., Brett W. Hawkins, and Stephen D. Edwards. 1969. "The Persistence of Ethnic Voting in Urban and Rural Areas: Results from the Controlled Election Method." *Social Science Quarterly* 49:891-99.

Lowi, Theodore J. 1964. *At the Pleasure of the Mayor*. New York: The Free Press.

Lubell, Samuel A. 1956. *The Future of American Politics*, 2nd ed. Garden City, NJ: Doubleday.

Luconi, Stefano. 1997. "Municipal Reforms and the Representation of Italian-Americans in the Local Administrations of Philadelphia and Pittsburgh." *Studi Emigrazione/Etudes Migrations* 34(125):61-82.

Magnum, Garth L. 1989. *Youth and America's Future.* Washington, DC: William T. Grant Foundation Commission on Work, Family, and Citizenship.

Marinho, Rita Duarte and Elmer E. Cornwell. 1992. *Os Luso-Americanos No Processo Politico Americano: Estudo Duma Situação Concreta.* Angra do Heroismo: Gabinete de Emigração e Apoio às Comunidades Açorianas.

Marcson, Simon. 1950. "A Theory of Intermarriage and Assimilation." *Social Forces* 24:75-8.

Marcson, Simon. 1951. "Intermarriage and Generational Status." *Phylon* (1) 2:357-63.

Massachusetts AFL-CIO. 1998. *Work and Family: Putting People First; Labor's Public Policy Agenda for Massachusetts in 1998 and Beyond.* Boston: Labor Resource Center, University of Massachusetts Boston.

Masssachusetts Department of Education. 1999. *Foreign Language Curriculum Framework.* Malden, MA. http://www.doe.mass.edu/frameworks/

Massachusetts Department of Education. 1999. *School and District Profiles 1998 - 1999.* http://www.doe.mass.edu/pic.www/pic.html.

Massachusetts Secretary of the Commonwealth. 2000. "Massachusetts Registered Voter Enrollment, 1948-2000" http://www.state.ma.us/sec.ele.eleenr.enridx.htm

Massey, Douglas S. 1995. "The New Immigration and Ethnicity in the United States." *Population and Development Review* 21(3):631-52.

Mayo, Martha, ed. 1994. *Comunidade: The Portuguese Community in Lowell, 1905-1930.* Lowell, MA: Lowell Historical Society.

Mazzatenta, O. Louis. 1975. "New England's Little Portugal." *National Geographic* (January.)

McCarthy, Rebecca. 2000. "Portuguese Spoken Here: UGA Program Lures Hundreds of Students." *Atlanta Constitution,* February 10, p. B-3.

McDonald, Hellen G., and Pallassana R. Balgopal. 1998. "Conflicts of American Immigrants: Assimilate or Retain Ethnic Identity." *Migration World Magazine* 26(4):14-18.

McGuinn, Taro. 1998. *East Timor: Island in Turmoil.* Minneapolis: Lerner Publications.

McNeill, Elton B. 1961. *Human Socialization.* Belmont, CA: Wadsworth Publishing Co.

Medeiros, John, and Donna Huse, et al. 1981. "Vizinhança: Neighborhood." *Spinner: People and Culture in Southeastern Massachusetts* 1:6-25.

Merton, Robert K. 1941. "Intermarriage and the Social Structure: Fact and Theory." *Psychiatry.*361-74.

Meyerson, Martin, and Edward C. Banfield. 1955. *Politics, Planning and the Public Interest.* Glencoe, IL: The Free Press.

Miranda, Manuel R. 2000. *The Portuguese Making of America: Melungeon and Early Settlers of America.* Franklin, NC: Portuguese-American Research Foundation.

Mishel, Lawrence and Jared Bernstein. 1992. *Declining Wages for High School and College Graduates: Pay And Benefits Trends by Education, Gender, Occupation, and State, 1979-1991.* Washington, DC: Economic Policy Institute.

Modern Language Association of America. 1998. *Foreign Language Enrollments in United States Institutions of Higher Education.* New York. http://www.mla.org.

Moniz, Rita. 1973. "The Portuguese Community of New Bedford, Massachusetts: A Statement on Political Participation in Terms of Cultural Assimilation." Southeastern Massachusetts University. Typescript.

Moniz, Rita. 1975. "Assimilation and Ethnic Political Behavior: The Portuguese Community of New Bedford, Massachusetts." Brown University. Typescript.

Moniz, Rita. 1975. "Mayoral Election 1969--New Bedford, Massachusetts: A Case Study." Brown University. Typescript.

Moniz, Rita, and Arnold Howitt. 1976. "Ethnic Identity, Political Organization and Political Structure: The Cape Verdean Community." Harvard Discussion Papers.

Moniz, Rita, and Arnold Howitt. 1976. "Ethnic Identity, Political Organization and Political Structure: The Cape Verdean Community." Presented at the annual meeting of the American Political Science Association, Chicago, Illinois.

Moniz, Rita. 1976. "Ethnicity and Political Behavior: The Portuguese of New Bedford." Presented at the Meeting of the Center for the Portuguese-Speaking World Conference, University of Massachusetts Dartmouth, Dartmouth, Massachusetts.

Moniz, Rita. 1979. "The Portuguese of New Bedford, Massachusetts and Providence, Rhode Island: A Comparative Micro-analysis of Political Attitudes and Behavior." Ph.D. dissertation, Brown University.

Moniz, Rita. 1981. "The Politics of Portuguese in America." *Portuguese-Times.* Twelve-part series.

Moore, Craig L. and Edward Moscovitch. 1994. *The New Economic Reality: Massachusetts Prospects for Long-Term Growth.* Boston: Massachusetts Taxpayers Foundation.

Moore, John Bassett. *Digest of International Law.* Vol. IV., Sect. 534-578

Morris, Richard T. and Melvin Seeman. 1950. "The Problem of Leadership: An Interdisciplinary Approach." *American Journal of Sociology* 56:149-55.

Mulcahey, Maria Da Gloria. 1998. "Portuguese Spinner – An American Story," in Marsha McCabe and Joseph D. Thomas, eds., *Portuguese Spinner, 1998*. New Bedford, MA:Spinner Publications.

Murphy, Ruth, and Sonja Blumenthal. 1966. "The American Community and the Immigrant." *Annals of the American Academy of Political and Social Science* 367:115-26.

Myers, Jerome K. 1957. "Assimilation in the Political Community." *Sociology and Social Research* 33(3):175-82.

Nagel, Joane, ed. 1986. *Competitive Ethnic Relations*. Orlando: Academic Press.

Nahirny, V., and J. A. Fishman. 1965. "American Immigrant Groups: Ethnic Identification and the Problem of Generations." *Sociological Review* 13:311-26.

National Center for Education Statistics. 1999. *The Condition of Education 1998*. Washington, DC: Government Printing Office.

National Commission on Excellence in Education. 1983. *A Nation At Risk: The Imperative for Educational Reform*. Washington, DC: U.S. Department of Education.

National Election Studies. 2000. "Times-Series Studies, 1952-1998." Ann Arbor: University of Michigan.

Neidert, Lisa J., and Reynolds Farley. 1985. "Assimilation in the United States: An Analysis of Ethnic and Generation Differences in Status and Achievement." *American Sociological Review* 50:840-50.

Nelli, Humbert S. 1970. *Italians in Chicago, 1890-1930*. New York: Oxford Press.

New Bedford High School Year Books. 1916-1976. New Bedford, MA: New Bedford School Department.

Newman, William M. 1973. *American Pluralism: A Study of Minority Groups and Social Theory*. New York: Harper & Row Publishers.

Nichols, Edith A. 1940. "Woman Visitor From Azores is Dazzled by Freedom of Her Sex in United States." *Providence Journal,* February 27, p. 13.

Nie, Norman H., Sydney Verba, and John R. Petrocik. 1976. *The Changing American Voter.* Cambridge, MA: Harvard University Press.

Noivo, Edite. 1993. "Ethnic Families and the Social Injuries of Class Migration, Gender, Generation and Minority Group Status." *Canadian Ethnic Studies* 25:66-75.

Novak, Michael. 1971. *The Rise of the Unmeltable Ethnics.* New York: Macmillan & Co.

Office of the President. 1997. *Economic Report of the President.* Washington, DC: United States Government Printing Office.

Oliveira, Benvinda, and Lucillia Lima (interviewer). 1981. "Lembrança: Crioulo Memories." *Spinner: People and Culture in Southeastern Massachusetts* 1:92-5.

Olzak, Susan. 1986. *Competitive Ethnic Relations.* Orlando: Academic Press.

Pap, Leo. 1981. *The Portuguese-Americans.* Boston: Twayne.

Parenti, Michael. 1967. "Ethnic Politics and the Persistence of Ethnic Identification." *American Political Science Review* 61:717-26.

Parreira, Miguel Abreu de Castro. 1971-5. "Portuguese Immigration in North America: Social History and Linguistic Considerations." *Boletim do Instituto Historico da Ilha Terceira* 29-33:9-166.

Patterson, Thomas E. 1980. *The Mass Media Election: How Americans Choose Their President.* New York: Praeger.

Pienkos, Angela T., ed. 1978. *Ethnic Politics in Urban America: The Polish Experience in Four Cities.* Chicago: Polish American Historical Association.

Pomper, Gerald. 1966. "Ethnic and Group Voting in Non-partisan Municipal Elections." *Public Opinion Quarterly* 30:79-97.

Porter, Michael. 1990. *The Competetive Advantage of Nations.* New York: Free Press.

Porter, Michael. 1991. *The Competetive Advantage of Massachusetts.* Boston: Secretary of the Commonwealth.

Portes, Alejandro, and Rafael Mozo. 1985. "The Political Adaptation Process of Cubans and Other Ethnic Minorities in the United States: A Preliminary Analysis." *International Migration Review* 19:35-63.

"Portuguese Form R.I. State Portuguese American Civic League." 1936. *Providence Journal,* April 28, p. 11.

"Portuguese-American Social Club Elects Joseph I. Mello, President." 1947. *Providence Journal,* January 6, p. 4.

Pressman, Jeffrey L. 1972. "Preconditions of Mayoral Leadership." *American Political Science Review* 66:511-24.

Prothro, James W., and C. W. Grigg. 1960. "Fundamental Principles of Democracy: Bases of Agreement and Disagreement." *Journal of Politics* 22:278-94.

Putnam, Robert D. 1993. *Making Democracy Work.* Princeton: Princeton University Press.

Putnam, Robert D. 1995. "Bowling Alone: America's Declining Social Capital." *Journal of Democracy* 6 (January): 65-78.

Putnam, Robert D. 2000. *Bowling Alone: The Collapse and Revival of American Community.* New York: Simon and Schuster.

Ramos, Lucy, and John C. Reardon (interviewer). 1981. "Black, White or Portuguese: A Cape Verdean Dilemma." *Spinner: People and Culture in Southeastern Massachusetts* 1:34-7.

Rapoza, Kenneth. 2000. "From the Mouths of Babes: Portuguese Kids Study Portuguese." *Boston Globe,* July 16, p. G5.

Reed, Robert D., and Danek S. Kaus. 1993. *Finding Your Portuguese-American Roots: A Guide to Researching Your Ethnic-American Cultural Heritage.* San Jose, CA: R&E Publishers, Inc.

Ribeiro, Jose Luis. 1982. *Portuguese Immigrants and Education.* Bristol, RI: Portuguese American Federation.

Reidy, Chris. 1994. "Portuguese Protest by Dropping Cable." *Boston Globe,* May 13, p. 77, col. 3.

Reynolds, H. T. 1974. *Politics and the Common Man: An Introduction to Political Behavior.* Homewood, IL: Dorsey Press.

Riding, Alan. 1991. "From the Pure of Tongue, Catcalls in Portuguese." *New York Times,* February 15, Sec. A, p. 4.

Rischin, Moses. 1960. *Our Own Kind: Voting by Race, Creed or National Origin.* Santa Barbara, CA: Center for the Study of Democratic Institutions.

Rodrigues, Rosa P. 1990. *Occupational Mobility of Portuguese Males in New Bedford, Massachusetts, 1870-1900.* New York: New School for Social Research, Ph.D. disseration.

Rogers, Francis M. 1974. "Americans of Portuguese Descent: A Lesson in Differentiation." In *Sage Research Papers in the Social Sciences, Studies in Ethnicity and Religion Series,* No. 90-013. Beverly Hills: Sage Publications.

Rogers, George. 1974. Interview. New Bedford, Massachusetts, December.

Rogler, Lloyd H. 1974. "The Changing Role of a Political Boss in a Puerto Rican Migrant Community." *American Sociological Review* 39:57-67.

Rollins, Joan H. ed. 1981. *Hidden Minorities: The Persistence of Ethnicity in American Life.* Washington, DC: University Press of America.

Rosa Borges, Aluisio Medeiros da. 1990. *The Portuguese Working Class in the Durfee Mills of Fall River, Massachusetts: A Study of the Division of Labor, Ethnicity, and Labor Union Partipation, 1895-1925.* State University of New York at Binghamton, Ph.D. dissertation.

Rose, Peter Issac. 1964. *They and We: Racial and Ethnic Relations in the United States.* New York: Random House.

Rosen, Ellen Israel. 1985. "The New Bedford Rape Trial: New Thoughts on an Old Problem." *Dissent* 32:207-12.

Rosenbaum, Alan. 1973. "Machine Politics, Class Interests, and the Urban Poor." Presented at the Meeting of the American Political Science Association.

Rosenfeld, Michael J. 1997. "The Mexican American Electoral Generation." Paper presented at the Meeting of the American Sociological Association.

Rosenthal, Eric. 1960. "Acculturation without Assimilation? The Jewish Community of Chicago, Illinois." *American Journal of Sociology* 66:275-87.

Ross, Edward A. 1913. *The Old World in the New.* New York: The Century Co.

Rumbaut, Ruben. 1999. "Immigration Research in the United States: Social Origins and Future Orientations." *American Behavioral Scientist* 42:1285-1301.

Ryan, Joseph ed. 1973. *White Ethnics: Their Life in Working Class America.* Englewood Cliffs, NJ: Prentice-Hall, Inc.

Salisbury, Robert H. 1969. "An Exchange Theory of Interest Groups." *Midwest Journal of Political Science* (13):1-32.

Saloutos, Theodore. 1964. *The Greek in the United States.* Cambridge: Harvard University Press.

Salvador, Mari L. 1990. *Festas Acoreanas: Portuguese Religious Celebrations in California and the Azores.* Lanham, MD: University Publishing Associates, Inc.

San Juan, Karin Aguilar, ed. 1994. *The State of Asian America: Activism and Resistance in the 1990s.* Boston: South End Press.

Sanchez, George J. 1999. "Race and Immigration History." *American Behavioral Scientist* 42:1271-75.

Santos, Robert L. 1996. "Azoreans to California: A Passionate People's Immigrant Song." *Californians* 13:30-1, 34-48.

Schermerhorn, R. A. 1970. *Comparative Ethnic Relations: A Framework for Theory and Research.* New York: Random House.

Schlesinger, Arthur M. 1925. *Political and Social History of the United States—Vol. I (1829-1925).* New York: The Macmillan Co.

Schwartz, Abba P. 1968. *The Open Society.* New York: William Morrow & Co., Inc.

Schwartz, David C. 1973. *Political Alienation and Political Behavior.* Chicago: Aldine Publishing Co.

Sessler, Amy. 1991. "Portuguese Culture, Other Communities Prosper in Peabody." *Boston Globe,* May 26, sec. N, p. 1.

Sharkansky, Ira. 1960. "The Portuguese of Fall River: A Study of Ethnic Acculturation." Honors Thesis, Wesleyan University.

Shefter, Martin. 1969. "The Emergence of the Political Machine: New York City, 1884-1897, as a Test Case." Typescript, Columbia University.

Shim, Jae K., and Joel G. Siegel. 1995. *Dictionary of Economics.* New York: John Wiley and Sons, Inc.

Shockley, John S. 1974. *Chicano Revolt in a Texas Town.* Notre Dame, IN: University of Notre Dame Press.

Showman, Daniel. 1968. *America Since 1920.* New York: Harper & Row Publishers.

Silva, John, Jr. 1969. *Azoreans in America and Americans in the Azores.* Bristol, RI: Portuguese-American Federation.

Silvestri, George T. and John M. Lukasiewicz. 1987. "Projections 2000: A Look at Occupational Employment Trends to the Year 2000." *Monthly Labor Review,* Vol. 110, no. 9 (September): 46-69.

Silvia, Philip T., Jr. 1973. "The Spindle City: Labor, Politics and Religion in Fall River, Massachusetts, 1870-1905." Ph.D. dissertation, Fordham University.

Silvia, Philip T., Jr. 1973. *The Spindle City: Labor, Politics, and Religion in Fall River,* 1870-1905, 2 Vols. New York: P.T. Silvia.

Slonin, Morris J. 1960. *Sampling in a Nutshell.* New York: Simon & Schuster, Publishers.

Smith, Robert C. 1988. "Sources of Urban Ethnic Politics: A Comparison of Alternative Explanations." *Research in Race and Ethnic Relations* 5:159-91.

Smothers, Ronald. 1997. "In Newark's Museum, An Exhibit Honors the City's Portuguese." *New York Times,* December 4, sec. B, p. 15.

Solomon, Barbara M. 1956. *Ancestors and Immigrants.* Cambridge: Harvard University Press.

Spiro, Milford E. 1955. "The Acculturation of American Ethnic Groups." *American Anthropologist* 57: 1240.

Stafford, Len. 1998. "Portuguese Community Has Annual Picnic Day." *Atlanta Journal Constitution,* June 14, Sec. C, p. 9.

Steger, Manfred B. 2001. *Globalism: The New Market Ideology.* Lanham, MD: Rowman and Littlefield.

Stephenson, George M. 1926. *A History of American Immigration.* Boston: Ginn and Co.

Sum, Andrew, and W. Neal Fogg. 1999. *The Changing Workforce: Immigrants and the New Economy in Massachusetts.* Boston: Massachusetts Institute for a New Commonwealth.

Suro, Roberto. 1995/96. "Hispanic Immigration: Beyond the Melting Pot and the Mosaic." *Responsive Community* 6 (Winter): 41-8.

Suro, Roberto. 1998. *Strangers Among Us: How Latino Immigration is Transforming America.* New York: Alfred A. Knopf.

Taft, Donald R. 1923. *Two Portuguese Communities in New England.* New York: Columbia University Press.

Tamotsu, Shibutani, and Kian M. Kwan. 1965. *Ethnic Stratification: A Comparative Approach.* New York: McMillan Co.

Tavares, Evelina. 1973. *Portuguese Pioneers in the United States.* Fall River, MA: R.E. Smith Printing Co.

Teixeira, Ruy, and Joel Rogers. 2000. *America's Forgotten Majority: Why the White Working Class Still Matters.* New York: Basic Books.

Treudley, Mary B. 1949. "Formal Organization and the Americanization Process with Special Reference to the Greeks of Boston." *American Sociological Review* 14:44-53.

Treudley, Mary B. 1953. "The Ethnic Group as a Collectivity." *Social Forces* 31:261-4.

Uhlaner, Carole J., Bruce E. Cain, and Roderick D. Kiewiet. 1989. "Political Participation of Ethnic Minorities in the 1980s." *Political Behavior* 11(3):195-231.

Ungar, Sanford J. 1995. *Fresh Blood: The New American Immigrants.* New York: Simon and Schuster.

United States Bureau of the Census. 2000. "Profile of General Demographic Characteristics for Massachusetts." http://www.census.gov/Press-Release/www/2001/tables/dpma1990.pdf

United States Bureau of the Census. 1999. *Statistical Abstract of the United States.* Washington, DC: Government Printing Office.

United States Department of Education. 1983. *National Commission on Excellence in Education.* Washington, DC.

United States Department of Labor. 1993. *Teaching the SCANS Competencies.* Washington, DC: Secretary's Commission on Achieving Necessary Skills.

205

United States International Trade Commission. 1998. *Annual Statistical Report on U.S. Imports of Textiles and Apparel: 1997,* Publication 3102. Washington, DC.

United States International Trade Commission. 1998. *The Year in Trade: Operation of the Trade Agreements Program During 1997.* Washington D.C.: USITC Publication 3103.

Verba, Sidney, and Norman H. Nye. 1972. *Participation in American Political Democracy and Social Equality.* New York: Harper and Row.

Vespa, Mary. 1984. "No Town Without Pity: A Divided New Bedford Seeks Justice in a Brutal Gang Rape Case." *People Weekly,* March 12, p. 77.

Victor, Diana. 2000. "UMass Study Looks at Portuguese Voting and Social Views." *O Jornal,* October 25, pp. 1, 10.

Victor, Diana. 2000. "A final, 'quem são os Portugueses?" *O Jornal,* November 1, pp. 1-2.

Vilella, Ruy S. 1975. Interview. New Bedford, Massachusetts, January 3.

Vlachos, Evangelos C. 1968. *The Assimilation of Greeks in the United States.* New York: Athens Press.

Wallerstein, Immanuel. 1960. "Ethnicity and National Integration." *Cahiers d'Etudes Africaines,* 1:131.

Walton, Hanes Jr. 1997. *African American Power and Politics: The Political Context Variable.* New York: Columbia University Press.

Warrin, Donald. 1997-98. "An Immigrant Path to Social Mobility: Portuguese Atlantic Islanders in the California Sheep Industry." *California History* 76:94-107.

Warrin, Donald. 1992. "Portuguese Pioneers in Early Nevada." *Nevada Historical Society* Quarterly 35(1):40-57.

Weinstein, Michael G., Peter T. Manicas, and Joseph J. Leon. 1990. "The Portuguese and Haoles of Hawaii." *American Sociological Review* 55:305-8.

Weinstock, S. Alexander. 1969. *Acculturation and Occupation.* Nyhoff: The Hague.

Weinstock, S. Alexander. 1964. "Some Factors that Retard or Accelerate the Rate of Acculturation, with Special Reference to Hungarian Immigrants." *Human Relations* 17(4):321-40.

Wessell, B. B. 1931. *An Ethnic Survey of Woonsocket, Rhode Island.* Chicago: University of Chicago Press.

Whyte, William F. Street. 1955. *Street Corner Society,* 2nd ed. Chicago: University of Chicago Press, 1955.

Wiarda, Ieda Siqueira. 1999. *Handbook of Portuguese Studies.* Philadelphia, PA: Xlibris Corporation.

Williams, Jerry R. 1982. *And Yet They Come: Portuguese Immigration from the Azores to the United States.* New York: Center for Migration Studies.

Williams, J. Allen, Jr., and Suzanne T. Ortega. 1990. "Dimensions of Ethnic Assimilation: An Empirical Appraisal of Gordon's Typology." *Social Science Quarterly* 71:697-710.

Williams, J. Allen, Jr., and Louis St. Peter. 1977. "Ethnicity and Socioeconomic Status as Determinants of Social Participation: A Test of the Interaction Hypothesis." *Social Science Quarterly* 57: 892-8.

Williams, J. Allen, Jr., Nicholas Babchuk, and David R. Johnson. 1973. "Voluntary Associations and Minority Status: A Comparative Analysis of Anglo, Black and Mexican Americans." *American Sociological Review* 38:637-46.

Wilson, James Q. 1961. "The Economy of Patronage." *Journal of Political Economy* 69:369-80.

Wilson, James Q. 1960. *Negro Politics: The Search for Leadership.* Glencoe, IL: The Free Press.

Wilson, James Q. 1973. *Political Organizations.* New York: Basic Books.

Wilson, James Q. 1960. "Two Negro Politicians." *Midwest Journal of Political Science* 4:346-9.

Wolfinger, Raymond E. 1974. *The Politics of Progress.* New York: Basic Books.

Wolfinger, Raymond E. and Steven J. Rosenstone. 1980. *Who Votes?* New Haven, CT: Yale University Press.

World Bank. 2000. *2000 World Development Indicators.* Washington, DC: International Bank for Reconstruction and Development.

Yancey, William L., Eugene P. Erickson, and Richard N. Juliani. 1976. "Emergent Ethnicity: A Review, and Reformulation." *American Sociological Review* 41:400.

Yetirian, Norman R., and C. Hoy Steele, eds. 1971. *Majority and Minority: The Dynamics of Racial and Ethnic Relations.* Boston: Allen & Bacon, Inc.

Yinger, J. Milton. 1961. "Social Forces Involved in Group Identification or Withdrawal." *Daedelus* 90 (2):247-62.

Zia, Helen. 2000. *Asian-American Dreams: The Emergence of an American People.* New York: Farrar, Straus, and Giroux.

Zubryski, Jerzy. 1958. "The Role of the Foreign Language Press in Migrant Integration." *Population Studies* 12: 73-82.

Dr. Clyde W. Barrow received his Ph.D. in Political Science from the University of California at Los Angeles in 1984. Dr. Barrow specializes in political economy and public policy. He is currently a professor at the University of Massachusetts, Dartmouth and has served as Director of the institution's Center for Policy Analysis since 1993. Dr. Barrow has published 4 books, 8 book chapters, and 47 articles in scholarly journals. His most recent publications are *Globalisation, Trade Liberalisation, and Higher Education in North America* (forthcoming 2003) and *Economic Impacts of the Textile and Apparel Industries in Massachusetts* (2000). Dr. Barrow serves as the Southeastern Massachusetts and Cape Cod regional analyst for the Massachusetts Benchmarks Project, which is co-sponsored by the University of Massachusetts Office of the President and the Federal Reserve Bank of Boston. The Benchmarks Project monitors the Massachusetts economy on a statewide and regional basis and publishes a quarterly journal that is distributed to business and government leaders. He is also the co-principal investigator and co-author with David Borges of a bi-weekly series in *The Sunday Standard-Times,* entitled "SouthCoast Signals,"which is a multi-year partnership between UMass Dartmouth and the Community Foundation of Southeastern Massachusetts to track 50 indicators that measure the overall economic, social, civic, physical, and environmental well-being of residents in the SouthCoast.

David Borges is a Senior Research Associate at the Center for Policy Analysis at UMass Dartmouth and is head of the Center's Education Division. He holds a Bachelor's degree in Political Science from UMass Dartmouth and a Master's degree in Public Administration from the University of Central Florida. His areas of expertise include survey research, program evaluation, and economic impact analysis. Published articles include *Regional Commercial Airports: Governance and Marketing,* published by the ICMA and *Education and Economic Development* published in the SouthCoast Insider. SouthCoast Signals is a bi-weekly series published in *The Sunday Standard-Times.* Mr. Borges is the co-author of a bi-weekly series, entitled "SouthCoast Signals," that is published by *The Standard-Times.* SouthCoast Signals is a multi-year analysis of 50 indicators selected to measure the overall economic, social, civic, physical, and environmental well-being of Massachusetts SouthCoast residents.

Rita Duarte Marinho, Ph.D. is Dean of the School of Humanities and Social Sciences at Millersville University. A summa cum laude graduate of the University of Massachusetts Dartmouth, she taught political science and women's studies there for more than two decades where she also held several administrative positions. A community activist she has served on the boards of many organizations including the national board of the YWCA and the Portuguese-American Women's Association. She also served on the New Bedford MA City Council. She is the author of many articles on the politics of the Portuguese-American communities of southeastern Massachusetts and Rhode Island. With Dr. Elmer E. Cornwell, Jr. of Brown University where Dr. Marinho received her Master's and Ph.D., she co- authored, *Portuguese-Americans and American Politics.*

Shawna E. Sweeney is a Senior Research Associate at the Center for Policy Analysis at UMass Dartmouth. She holds a Bachelor's degree in Political Science from UMass Dartmouth (magna cum laude), a Master's degree in Political Science from SUNY Binghamton, and is completing her doctoral dissertation in international political economy at SUNY Binghamton. Her areas of expertise include economic impact analysis, program evaluation, statistical analysis, and management/coordination of public forums and international conferences. Published articles include *Tourism and Regional Cooperation* (with Clyde W. Barrow) published in the SouthCoast Insider and *Conference Focuses on Oil Spill Policy Impact* published by the Oil Spill Intelligence Report. Ms. Sweeney also served as the Managing Editor for a special double issue of *Spill Science and Technology Bulletin* to be published in August 2002. SSTB is an international peer-reviewed journal on oil and chemical spill science and technology published by Elsevier Science Ltd. The special double issue, entitled "Media, Policy, and Regulation of Oil Spills," published a range of papers delivered at UMass' 1st International Conference on

Marine Environmental Challenges, held in February 2001, which was sponsored by SMAST and the Center for Policy Analysis. Ms. Sweeney served as the official Conference Coordinator for this important international forum.